The Shrew

PLAYSCRIPT 73

The Shrew

Freely adapted
from
William Shakespeare's
THE TAMING OF THE SHREW

by
CHARLES MAROWITZ

CALDER AND BOYARS · LONDON

First published in Great Britain in 1975
by Calder and Boyars Ltd
18 Brewer Street London W1R 4AS

© Charles Marowitz 1975

ISBN 0 7145 1118 8 Cased Edition

Typesetting by Gilbert Composing Services, Leighton Buzzard
and set in Press Roman
Printed by Whitstable Litho, Straker Brothers Ltd.

INTRODUCTION

It is generally accepted that today, Shakespeare can be reinterpreted for modern audiences either in the manner practised by the Royal Shakespeare and National Theatre companies, or in some more flamboyant or 'loose' way as, for instance, in the pop musical *Two Gentlemen Of Verona* or *Catch My Soul*, the rock version of *Othello*. Before 1960, it was common practice for directors to put new slants onto Shakespearian narratives, although a gentlemen's agreement existed in regard to the plays' original structures. Today, this agreement has been abrogated and many of Shakespeare's plays are used only as a kind of trampoline for modern directors and writers to perform what somersaults they choose. Apart from bouncing off of original Shakespearian works, there is also the practise of bouncing contemporary works off of Shakespeare—as in the cases of Tom Stoppard's *Rosencrantz and Guildenstern Are Dead* and Edward Bond's *Lear*.

In all of these convolutions, there is an underlying assumption that the new work, no matter how extrapolated, still owes some kind of debt to its original source and, indeed, in the more successful treatments, the spirit of the original can be discerned coursing through the coagulated matter from which the Frankenstein monster has been assembled.

The Victorians, who took their own liberties with Shakespeare, would probably be horrified at the excesses to which contemporary adaptors have gone to wrench new meanings from these standard sources. They would insist that their own pruning and revisions were, at least, born out of a deep-seated respect for Shakespeare and consisted of relatively minor changes compared to the sweeping overhauls of rock musicals or experimental collages. Technically, they would be quite right, but what is significant is the impulse, as rife today as it was in Victorian England, to doctor works which the main-stream public regard as classics. Not heeding Artaud's exhortations to destroy masterpieces, the contemporary tendency is to reassemble them by means of elaborate, sometimes outrageous surgery which may stop short of wholesale decimation but need not necessarily do so.

However, not all classical tinkering is aimed at sweep-ing overhauls. There is, for instance, the invisible mending which has become the stock-in-trade of John Barton at Stratford. Compressing the York-Lancaster cycle into the epic trilogy *The Wars of the Roses, (Henry VI, Richard III,* and the newly-fashioned *Edward IV),* Barton grafts together historically related plays and cunningly removes the joins. A new pattern emerges which provides a fresh perspective on each of the works used to make up the trilogy. Barton's Shakespearian pastiche, when it is concealing amendments, is thoroughly successful because the blending process is indiscernible. But when he grows bolder, as he did in the 1974 production of *King John* (versifying the conflicts of the Common Market) or his fanciful rewrite of Marlowe's *Doctor Faustus,* the mixture of Barton and the classics sour the palate.

In *Faustus* for instance, where refinement was clearly the objective, it requires a massive dose of insensitivity not to realize that a new scene filled with sexual innuendoes employing contemporary puns only highlights the appearance of alien material. Quite apart from being gauche, in no less a degree than the pseudo-comic gaucheries of the original, Faustus' overt amours with the Duchess of Anholt (Barton contributes an explicit seduction scene), gives the character a brashness which clearly belies the philosopher's sexual timidity and lack of initiation. However, the integration of scenes and exposition from the Faustbuch (first incorporated in my own adaptation of 1969) is judiciously handled and adds useful texture to a play whose small patches of Marlovian eloquence are too often swamped by its humourless gambols and crude sleights-of-hand. Barton's great skill is as editor and play-doctor, making pertinent amendments

6

and cross-references, applying plasters, effecting the occasional transplant and, in almost every case, fortifying the original work.

Bertolt Brecht's incursions into the classics are remarkable mainly because he chooses those plays which are already predisposed to his own ideology. It is a moot point which is the more radical play, Farquhar's *The Recruiting Officer* or *Trumpets and Drums,* Brecht's overstated version of it. (There is no question at all as to which is the better play.) The same question can be asked of *Coriolanus* which neon-lights a point about demagogic pride already well-illuminated by Shakespeare—but here, the finished work was done after Brecht's death and so is perhaps not a fair example. Brecht's adaptation of Marlowe's *Edward II,* in collaboration with Leon Feuchtwanger, emphasises the homosexual bond between Edward and Gaveston but is less politically sophisticated than Marlowe's original which underscores the background manoeuvres that actually determine the actions of the Crown. His version of *Antigone* is, again, a reduction-through-oversimplification. The play forfeits its moral balance by loading the dice against Creon. (Anouilh's treatment, due in large part to the time it first appeared in occupied France, actually adds new dimensions to Sophocles.) Brecht is much more effective when he cuts loose from the original source and follows his own bent. A play like *The Resistible Rise of Arturo Ui,* animated by the spirit of *Richard III,* imaginatively converts Shakespeare to Brechtian uses and is at once better Brecht and a more interesting form of classicial allusion. And *The Threepenny Opera,* compared to John Gay's *Beggar's Opera* which gave rise to it, is a staggering example of how a 20th century spirit can extend and elaborate an 18th century impulse, with each work enhancing the integrity of the other.

In passing, perhaps one should touch upon those Shakespearian adaptations which cut right across the works being discussed here; adaptations which, far from being experimental, are usually extremely commercial and thoroughly popular. Musicals such as *The Boys From Syracuse (*from *Comedy of Errors), Kiss Me Kate* (from *Taming of the Shrew), West Side Story* (from *Romeo*

and Juliet) and the aforementioned *Two Gentlemen Of
Verona* and *Catch My Soul* are basically riffs on their
originals using the basic story as a clothesline on which
to hang an assortment of fetching new attire. Being
expressly 'free' treatments specifically designed to change
the medium of expression, they have a different set of
priorities from a work which deals with the intellectual
structure of the original play and confines itself, more
or less, to the given material. Being preoccupied with the
additions of song, dance and updated comedy, the
musicals make use only of the myth of the originals, the
generally accepted gist of the plays rather than their
actual units. But the fact remains that in a work like *Kiss
Me Kate* for instance, what is compulsive, quite as much
as the singing and dancing, is the developing narrative
line about a temperamental actress and an actor attempting to subdue her will. Also, there is a cunning aptness
about a Kate who is a prima donna and a Petruchio who
personifies theatrical egotism. One is clearly, if sub-
terraneously, being nourished by the original play. In
West Side Story, the sense of warring communities, violent
bigotry and victimized lovers is every whit as potent as it
is in *Romeo and Juliet*—which is not to draw irrelevant
comparisons, but only to point out that when the
contemporary parallels have a direct pipeline to the
actions on which they are based, the new work rests on a
solid foundation and, resting so, can build upwards as far
as it likes. *The Boys From Syracuse* takes little more than
the idea of confused identities from *Comedy of Errors,*
which Shakespeare himself lifted from the *Menaechmi,*
but this buoyant Rodgers and Hart musical is thoroughly
imbued with the zaniness that Shakespeare extracted from
Plautus. *(A Funny Thing Happened on the Way to the
Forum* owes a similar debt.)

Catch My Soul is already a different species, being
more a rock recital inspired by the alleged funkiness of
the Moor than a full-fledged musical comedy treatment
depending upon character and developing situation. The
original story is, as it were, 'quoted' while singers and
dancers project a variety of obliquely related musical
numbers which simultaneously oversimplify and
overintensify the ingredients of the play; which is to say,

they respond to the imperatives of amplified rock music rather than those of the drama.

As a tendency, musicalized Shakespeare is full of potential and to be encouraged. But the underlying principles are exactly the same as those which apply to Brecht or anyone else. In order to derive value from the original, new dimensions with contemporary substance have to be uncovered or imposed. It is leaden and deadly simply to 'set Shakespeare to music' without some organizing drive that justifies and ultimately enriches the media change. *Kiss Me Kate,* by embracing the spirit of *Taming of the Shrew,* leaves Shakespeare in credit. *Catch My Soul,* by musically paraphrasing only the narrative elements in *Othello,* confers no great distinction either to Shakespeare or itself. When Shakespeare appropriated Boccacio or Holinshed, it was always in the name of that rampaging personal egotism that was ultimately responsible for the transformation and improvement of the sources from which he borrowed.

In all of these unrelated activities, each adaptor has his own intentions and priorities, and any attempt to bring them into line, to foist a generalization wide enough to cover say Brecht's *Coriolanus* and Jerome Robbins' *West Side Story,* must produce one of those phoney definitions to which academics are so prone: a kind of new nomenclature which, once devised, is employed to bend a multitude of divergent tendencies into something like an orderly system. The result of these stretched critical tendons is to create a sense of uprightness where none exists. And so to avoid this pitfall, I shall say from the start that I speak for no one but myself, and that no matter how dogmatic my tone may become, I do not presume that my work is the frontrunner of any kind of *zeitgeist*—nor do I propagate it in order to attract converts.

Since about 1956, I have had a curious love-hate relationship with certain old plays—mostly those of Shakespeare—and in the past ten years or so have found myself dealing with them in various ways. What all of this portends I really do not know, but what I do know, and what is very often lost sight of, is that my experi-

9

ments have been conducted in a very small arena (usually a London theatre seating a maximum of 200 persons) and that most of the other classical innovations have likewise been directed to a very small public, so that whatever 'tendency' is being delineated here, it affects only very slightly the ways in which the majority of theatregoers receive the works of Shakespeare.

The first exercise of mine along these lines was the direct result of conversations with Peter Brook in which we discussed the possibilities of conveying theatrical meaning without reliance on narrative. Would it be possible, we conjectured, to convey the multitude of nuances and insights which are to be found in *Hamlet* through a kind of cut-up of the work which thoroughly abandoned its progressive story line? If the story proper would not be conveyed through such a drastic reassembly, what would? The result was a twenty-eight minute collage stitched together from random sections of the play and wedged into an arbitrary structure (*viz.* the soliloquy 'How all occasions to inform against me').* The intention to fragment the work and then play it discontinuously forced us to devise a performance technique which would project such a collage form. This was in many ways a more fascinating problem than the assembly of the work itself, for it encouraged the actors to forego all the conventional means by which they usually achieved their effects. Nothing could *build,* for instance, for longer than two or three minutes; no scene could *develop* to a logical conclusion because no scene ever concluded but was abruptly intersected by another, invariably with a different texture and from another part of the play. The sustenance of character became secondary to the transmutation of character as a result of jumps in time and location. The collage was eventually extended to eighty minutes after which time the pressure of discontinuity became almost unbearable.

It became fashionable to say that if you already knew *Hamlet,* this was a fascinating rescension which would provide a kind of salutary shock. But the fact is the

* *The Marowitz Hamlet,* London: Penguin, 1968; also contains adaptation of Marlowe's *Doctor Faustus.*

collage was played before hundreds of people who had never read *Hamlet* or seen the film, and their impressions (derived from discussions after the performance) were as valid, and often as knowledgeable, as those of scholars and veteran theatregoers. I had always contended that the ideas contained in the collage were derived from Shakespeare's original and could be transferred back to a straightforward production of the play proper. In Gothenberg and then again in Wiesbaden, I had the opportunity to put that theory to the test. Whatever my misgivings about each production, what became abundantly clear was that every notion which seemed so farfetched in the context of the collage, was viable in terms of the original work and could be conveyed through conventional interpretation. Which begs the question: why cut it up in the first place?

In my view, radical theatrical experiments need to be justified, if at all, only when they fail. The *Hamlet* collage was, on the whole, successful, and earned a certain credibility of its own. But if one were hard pressed for justification, I would say that the re-structuring of a work, the characters and situations of which are widely known, is an indirect way of making contact with that work's essence. Just as the human organism is understood differently when its metabolism is scrutinized in isolation, so certain 'classical' works are understood differently when their components are re-formed. This 'different understanding' is not only the result of a new vantage-point (although this advantage should not be underestimated), but the consequence of changing the play's time-signature. A collage form bequeaths speed, and when you have the advantage of speed in the theatre (without, one must add, the loss of definition), not only do you change the nature of what is being said, you also change the purpose for saying it. Shakespeare's Aristotelian dramatic format obliged him to 'unfold' stories, 'develop' characters and 'illustrate' themes. But a collage-version of a known play assumes a pre-knowledge of the original and although it tends to cover familiar ground (refers to characters, alludes to situations, comments on themes), it is more concerned with the application of all these things in order to foster another concept. If the old

11

material was not being redistributed for the sake of this other concept, the collage-form would simply be another way of cutting meat; a stylistic mechanism which rearranged material simply for the sake of rearranging it. The change of form inescapably affects the nature of content, but that in itself is not enough. The content must not be accidentally 'affected' in the way that a pedestrian might be 'affected' if he were hit by a bus. It must be refashioned as if, to pursue the metaphor, a pedestrian were hit by a bus driven by a clinical psychiatrist whose aim in knocking him down was to investigate his rate of recovery in response to highly-specialized therapies of his own making. Which is a circuitious way of saying that a collage must have a purpose as coherent and proveable as any conventional work-of-art.

Apart from the stylistic techniques deployed in the *Hamlet* collage, I attempted to delineate a criticism of the type of person Hamlet was and, by inference, to indict the values which he represented; values which (i.e. misdirected moral concern, intellectual analyses as action-substitute, etc.) were, in my view, disreputable in our society and which derived much of their respectability and approval from traditional works such as Shakespeare's *Hamlet.* In short, by assaulting the character of Hamlet, one was deriding the supreme prototype of the conscience-stricken but paralysed liberal; one of the most lethal and obnoxious characters in modern times.

I now accept that the stylistic innovations in the work were so overwhelming it was difficult to insinuate this idea very lucidly, and I fully accept the fact that most of the public which responded to the collage were more taken with its theatricality than its thesis; but without that thesis, none of that theatricality would have had any coherent motive nor, as I have already said, any purpose. I derive some small consolation from the fact that any artefact which is immediately reducible to its theoretical components must be facile and unworthy, but am simultaneously chastened by the knowledge that many artists imagine they are communicating clear-cut intentions when in fact, they are conveying something entirely ambiguous which, being approved for unexpected reasons, persuades them (hypocritically) to relinquish

12

their original demands in regard to their work.

In *Macbeth**, as with *Hamlet,* the collage treatment had the intention of transmitting experience from the play through the eyes of the central protagonist. The technique was more appropriate in *Macbeth* because one had decided to forage about in the black magical undergrowth that lay behind the work, and a fragmented structure helped to create the desired nightmarish effect. But again, one was putting an interpretation suggested by the play itself: Macbeth, victim of a witchcraft plot masterminded by Lady Macbeth (the chief witch of a coven which included the three witches), progressively destroyed by forces he could not envisage and therefore not understand, is, for me, a construction direct from Shakespeare's work. The intense paranoia of the man in the final stages of dissolution is remarkably like the hallucination of one possessed. 'Possession' vibrates through every page of the original play from Lady Macbeth's murderous preoccupation with Duncan, to Banquo's obsession with the witches' prophecy, to Macduff's all-consuming dream of revenge— not to mention the overriding spell with which Lady Macbeth confounds her husband and monitors him towards acts which, after her own madness, seem difficult to accept merely as the cunning ploys of an ambitious wife.

One also tried to dramatize the peculiar knot of trinities that winds its way through the play; three witches, three murderers, three murders; hence in the collage, three personified aspects of Macbeth, the Timorous, the Ambitious, the Nefarious. One tried to restore the play to its pre-Christian, Manichean origins; tried to locate its metaphysical centre and peel away the pseudo-religious and irrelevantly-political gauzes that had woven themselves around the work.

Having said all that I must also add that for me, *Macbeth* was always something of a bloodless exercise in cut-up techniques. The excitements of the collage-format happened organically in *Hamlet,* aided by the fact that there were so many disparate pieces to put together in new and unexpected ways. The redistribution of its parts

* *A Macbeth,* London: Calder & Boyars. 1971

was like a multifarious recipe which incorporated many different ingredients. But cutting up *Macbeth* was a little like slicing salami. However one changed its structure (in fact, there was very little change), one was always left with that dark-textured, relentlessly plot-laden Warner Brothers movie about the man who rubbed out Mr. Big and, perforce, had to continue to rub out all the other members of the mob. Clearly, Shakespeare's *Macbeth* has none of the rambling paths and hidden rivulets of *Hamlet.* In its remorseless journey from crime to retribution, it is more like a motorway. Because its intellectual base is less complex than *Hamlet,* one becomes more aware of the technique qua technique. However, in the play's tumultuous coda where Macbeth's downfall is more labyrinthine and more terrible than any other of Shakespeare's tragic heroes, the collage-treatment provides an interior view of dissolution more vividly than one would get from the churn of a sequential narrative. Having lived inside of Macbeth's skin from the very start, the slow crumble of the spirit within that skin is, in some ways, more harrowing because more directly experienced. I say this not to draw snide comparisons with Shakespeare's original play, but to point out that the different vantage-point of a collage (i.e. an inside view of external developments) can alter the entire resonance of a theatrical experience. Of course, an ex-ray is not the same thing as a work of art, but an ex-ray *of* a work of art may claim to fall into a different category.

Unintentionally, *An Othello** marked a departure from the earlier adaptations by being a deliberate effort to impose new meaning which was flatly at odds with the play's original intentions.

Certain Jews always go to *The Merchant of Venice* expecting the character of Shylock to relate in some way to the 'Jewish Question', 'the Final Solution', and the past four centuries of Jewish repression. Of course, they are always frustrated because Shakespeare's play cannot possibly satisfy these expectations. Though this is acknowledged, the anticipations irrationally linger on.

* *'An Othello'*, in *Open Space Plays,* London: Penguin, 1974.

14

So it is with contemporary blacks coming to *Othello* expecting 'The Moor of Venice' to contain parallels to the racial strife of the past hundred years. But the incontrovertible fact about *Othello* is that it is an eloquent melodrama concerning a *crime passionel* and not at all about slavery, segregation or black repression. And yet the presence of the Jew in one play and the black in the other lures directors and audiences into forging associations between contemporary preoccupations and the period piece. Even as the conscious mind insists They do not relate, some unquenchable part of it is demanding, They ought to.

It was this desire to try to accommodate the black revolutionary spirit irrationally lodged in an audience's expectations that made me want to tackle *Othello,* and by 'tackle it', I mean by-pass Shakespeare's original intentions, extracting from the original only what I needed to achieve my own purposes. One proceeded from a series of impertinent questions directed towards the play and its central character: What is this black General doing at the head of a white army fighting Turks who, if not actually black, are certainly closer to his own race than his Venetian masters? Why is he the only black in the play? Are we to assume he is some kind of splendid oddity in an otherwise white society? That no racial tension exists in the State despite miscegenation, senatorial bigotry and wars waged against non-whites? (Obviously, these are not historically based speculations, but a series of false hypotheses, if you like, inspired by the need to re-programme the play according to new criteria.)

Othello, in a white context, is noble, courageous, forthright and commendable. But place one other black into that context and his credibility is immediately undermined. Fill it with thousands of members of an under-privileged black society and his position is morally untenable. In this new dispensation, Iago becomes a useful ploy. For centuries, critics have agreed that, given the enormity of his crime, the man lacks sufficient motivation. His claim of Emilia's infidelity with Othello is clearly implausible if for no other reason than because Shakespeare does not permit tragic heroes to fraternize

15

with low comic characters, except for comic relief. And if he wanted merely to rise in rank, he need not have exposed himself to all the dangers inherent in a murderous conspiracy. But if Othello is the epitome of the House Nigger (the conformist black), and Iago of the Field Nigger (the revolutionary black), then a legitimate motivation can be provided for Othello's destruction. And with this tool, I managed to make Iago subvert Othello at every turn—as a racial traitor, a political dupe, and a conformist actor in a potentially revolutionary context.

The original idea was simply to edit Shakespeare's text in order to bring out the theme of black-white conflict. After spending many useless weeks attempting this, I found myself writing one small piece which I felt was necessary to the new scheme. Little by little, more material got incorporated and more of the original got excised. When the script was finally completed, two thirds of it turned out to be original material derived from black writers or my own American experience, and one third, Shakespeare's original. It soon became clear that I had created two plays: one about the conformist and revolutionary tendencies in black America, and the other an indictment of the traditional conception of Othello. Since there was a connection between the two, I decided, rather than try to resolve the dichotomy, to implement one as the main theme and the other as the sub-plot—intertwining them when it became practical to do so. Again, a collage structure was utilized (to dramatize the welter of events streaming in Othello's mind during his epileptic fit), but this time it represented only a small part of the overall work, which was made up mainly of contrasting sections of verse and contemporary American dialogues.

To some aesthetes, this forced coupling of classical and contemporary elements is as insupportable as miscegenation is to southern American or South African whites. The charge, why not write your own play and leave Shakespeare's alone, would seem to be almost unanswerable in regard to *Othello.* And yet, one does answer it by pointing out that if one's intention is to grapple with the sub-conscious matter in a classical tragedy, the accretion of over four hundred years of history and culture, it serves no purpose to write a play about Little Rock. No contemporary drama, no matter how pungent, could have produced the dislocations and dis-orientations I wished to achieve with *Othello*. The question, as I see it, is not why not write one's own play, but how far can one gravitate from a known classic and still retain, as it were, radio-control with it? How many orbits is a work of art capable of? At what point in time does one sever the connection deliberately forged with a classic and, more interestingly, at what point does original authorship pass beyond the gravitational pull of the initiating work? For me, *An Othello* would be unthinkable without Shakespeare's work, and no matter how widely one ranges from it, the original play remains both the launch-pad and the recovery-vessel. If there is any value at all, it is purely in the distance travelled.

The Shrew had a premature delivery. The idea of converting Shakespeare's comedy into a gothic tragedy had been knocking around in my head for many months, and I always promised myself that one day I would sit down and think it all out. But in the winter of 1974, having promised the Hot Theatre in The Hague a production of Brecht's *The Messingkauf Dialogues,* one of those unexpected human-relations disasters struck The Open Space and, after one promising rehearsal, it was impossible to follow through on the Brecht project. Having already signed contracts for a date only three weeks away, I was exhorted by my partner Thelma Holt to 'pull something out of the bag'. I protested that mine was a very meagre, ordinary bag, not a magical rucksack, and one could not simply 'pull something out' without having first spent many months storing something up. As so often happens at The Open Space, the promise of a large sum of money and the theatre's desperately wobbly circumstances dislodged whatever block it was that made me insist we must cancel, and I hauled out my loosely-conceived Gothic *Shrew*. I outlined it to Thelma Holt and Nikolas Simmonds (both casting casualties from the abandoned Brecht work) and I was urged, more out of desperation than enthusiasm, to get on with it. The play, not yet written and only barely conceived, was cast within twenty-four hours and, in forty-eight hours, rehearsals began on a batch of hastily-assembled, photocopied sheets scrounged out of Shakespeare's play the night before.

The plan called for a young man and woman who would improvise a series of contemporary scenes roughly parallel to the Shakespearian ones derived from *The Taming of the Shrew.* Jeremy Nicholas and Kay Barlow, two very game actors who were as much in the dark as the director and adaptor, worked up a series of improvisations based on the courtship of a young working-class youth and upper middle-class girl. I siphoned off from these scenes enough juice to concoct some viable material and in the ensuing weeks, something was hashed together.

The thematic problems of *The Shrew* became clearer and clearer each time we played it. The parallel scenes were too baldly parallel to the Petruchio and Kate scenes, and the message that seemed to screech out of the modern scenes in which She (cum-Bianca) domineered and manipulated He (cum-Hortensio) was that nothing very much had changed since the 17th century; that cruelty and power-play were still the active components of relationships and that whereas, in the good old days, the man could brutalize the woman using physical means, today the woman could tyrannize the man using the more subtle weapons of psychology and social exploitation. Clearly, this was a statement not worth making—and certainly not worth cutting up a Shakespearian play in order to make. But the novelty of seeing *The Shrew* played as Grand Guignol was so enthralling to London audiences that the play had a hefty run at The Open Space, was revived, toured throughout England and ultimately wound up in Yugoslavia. Throughout all of these productions (there were three), I came to loathe the work I had done. It was no justification to explain that it had been done hastily and under great pressure. The result was intellectually contemptible and no

18

amount of superb playing by Thelma Holt and Nikolas Simmonds could alter my own jaundiced view of it.

My desire was to flush the play down the drain, to discard it as a hashed exercise in theatrical expediency; but the script continued to be requested on the continent, in America, in Australia and in Germany where I was invited to direct it at the Staatstheater in Stuttgart. It was then that I decided to 'do the right thing' by the work and tacitly resolved that the play performed in Stuttgart would be a revised, rethought and rewritten work. In short, I would do in Germany, with six full weeks of rehearsal, what I never had the time nor money to do in England. I would make the adaptation I had dimly conceived before the Dutch pressure brought the play prematurely into being.

This involved a careful reassessment of the play's ideology, or, rather, the ideology of the contemporary scenes—for this was where the trouble lay. I did not intend to say that things never change, that cruelty between human beings is a constant factor which only alters its methods but not its intentions. What I wanted to say was, in fact, much more dismal and depressing; namely: that no human relationship has the stamina to withstand long periods of intimate exposure; that familiarity not only breeds contempt but dissipation and stasis; that deep within the very fabric of human relationships, relationships founded on love and togetherness, there was an insidious canker which slowly but surely gnawed away at the euphoria that infused every love affair; that there was something at the core of human nature which was irrevocably abusing and self-consuming, and that the irony of this cancer was that it lurked quietly but potently in a context of love, watching love slowly corrode and growing gradually bolder and bolder until, ultimately, it conquered all. And, irony or ironies, it was at this very juncture that the diseased lovers often sought in the institution of marriage a kind of miracle drug which would transform everything. One wanted to show that for many people, despite the raging permissiveness of our times, Marriage, the hoked-up, endlessly-spoofed Magic Ritual, still held out a promise of salvation; a hope that an ancient ceremony could transform a grubby reality; that a solemn rite could, by virtue of its intrinsic ceremonial magic, right the wrongs of years.

To tell such a story, Shakespeare's combative couple had to leave the realms of farce and transmute themselves into a kind of Grimm Fairly Tale world, a world of sinister archetypes and hopeless victims. Petruchio, transformed into a kind of Mafiosa-monster who still covets Baptista's fortune   and is fully prepared to instigate a bloodless courtship to obtain it, is now motivated even more strongly by the detestable independence of spirit that throbs inside of Katherine. The confrontation between this Petruchio and this Kate is the classic encounter of elegance and vulgarity rather than female high-spiritedness and the urge for male sexual conquest. The tragedy of Kate, in this new dispensation, is that she underestimates the magnitude of Petruchio's bestiality. How could she not? The rich daughter of a rich father; the recipient of, if not love, then certainly luxury, education and breeding? Compare such a woman to a strolling fortune-hunter who goes sniffing for rich game and makes no distinction between material gain and amoristic conquest; for whom, indeed, the latter is only a means of acquiring the former. A wastrel, a bogus cavalier; a man who never read Castiglione but who knows the only way to get on in the world is to emulate his type. A man whose peculiar psychosis insists on total subservience as the emblem of love; who counterfeits with the grim, convincing deport-ment of the crypto-psychopath; who embodies and glories in all the characteristics Wilhelm Reich attributes to the Phallic-Narcissist.

The modern technique for brainwashing is, almost to the letter, what Petruchio makes Katherine undergo. Deprivation of food, deprivation of sleep, disorientation of faculties; cruelty camouflaged as kindness; a reversal of moral values which turns the tormentor into a holy man and the tormented into a hopeless sinner. Petruchio's evil genie punishes Katherine for the greatest crime of all—social rebellion. A woman she can be, she must be; but not *her* kind of woman—rather, the social cipher that

Baptista prefers, that Bianca unquestionably is, that Hortensio would have all women be, that Petruchio labours to create. If Katherine can be made to represent breeding and elegance, and one is able to discard the tirades of the traditional termagent, her downfall becomes truly pathetic, for it then represents the abandoment of personal style in the face of a brutalizing conformity. If she is shrilly vituperative and conventionally shrewish (Elizabeth Taylor swinging frying-pans), then all she receives is come-uppance and the conventional charade of subterranean longings for Petruchio clear the way for her wholesale conversion to domesticity; a conversion which, in my view, is never alleviated by a tang of irony in the final speech. Katherine accepts nothing and struggles against her cruel punishment to the very end. The only victory available to the Petruchio-Baptista-Bianca axis is the artificially induced spectacle of a mesmerized or drugged victim droning the words her tormentors could not make her speak voluntarily. A victory of these dimensions is hollow indeed.

What rots Katherine is the quicklime of Petruchio's spirit. What rots the contemporary Boy and Girl is the indeterminate moral pollution which many would blame on the social context but whose toxin is discharged through the pores of the human beings which constitute that society. There is no villain or villainess in the con-temporary scenes. Whatever personal failings the Boy and Girl may have, they are typical not unique. What happens to them happens to many people. Their 'tragedy', if you like, is built into their human metabolism. They can never escape, and their danger is never, like Katherine's, apparent and challengable. Katherine is felled by the will of a destructive force she can feel and see. She knows where to do battle and she does so valiantly—right up until the end. The Boy and Girl go through the motions of living and loving, of jealousy and possessiveness, of separations and reunions—like experimental mice that caper and cavort, feed and defecate, but whose destiny is sealed the moment they enter their laboratory cages. I am not alluding here to anything as simple as predestina-tion. Perhaps there *is* another way out for The Boy and

Girl; perhaps marriage will replenish their love-cells; but as we see them, they haven't the power to do anything more than feed off each other, try to elude boredom, hope for transformations in their inner lives, and, ultimately, settle for less—the inescapable 20th century compromise. The Boy and Girl have quarrels but Katherine fights for her life. The Boy and Girl dwindle into social statistics; Katherine's defeat defines the grandeur of a spirit that has been brought down by overwhelming odds. There is something noble in that defeat because in its resistance, an alternative way of life, a higher degree of individuality, has been implied. The Boy and Girl gradually disappear into the feckless, wholly expedient, mutually exploitative morass of modern life. It is hard to say, viewed that way, which represents the greater tragedy.

What eventually emerges from a survey of my own work and work similar to it, is that there are three basic requisites in regard to adaptations of this kind. Firstly, the director-adaptor has got to have something specific to say; that is, he has to shape his material in such a way that the new pattern, despite the existence of familiar source-material, delivers a quite specific and original message, a message which does not merely duplicate the statements of the *UR*-text. Secondly, the material, weighted as it is with the author's original intentions and the accumulation of four or more hundred years of fixed associations, has to have the elasticity to bend in the desired direction. It is when the nature of the contemporary comment goes against the grain of the given material that one usually winds up with those fractured, aberrant, wilfully *avant-garde* productions where minds, patently inferior to Shakespeare's, are trying to foist ideas which wilt in comparison. The third requirement is to recognize that when the ideas generated by the given material are not reconcilable with the work as it stands, it is politic to change the original rather than, out of respect or timidity, produce a set of clanging incompatibles. One should not back away from an idea which could not possibly have existed in Shakespeare's time if that idea has been inspired by Shakespeare's material. The resolution of what appear to be antithetical elements is often the first step towards the creation of a viable new form.

Ultimately, this kind of re-interpretation has little to do with 'new slants' on traditional material; it eschews the stunning nuances of unexpected verse delivery or the clever innuendoes of costume and set-design. It sets no premium on new approaches to characterization or novel forms of staging. It is nothing more nor less than a head-on confrontation with the intellectual sub-structure of the plays, an attempt to test or challenge, revoke or destroy the intellectual foundation which makes a classic the formidable thing it has become. Paradoxically, one can view this as a very traditional exercise. It does not annihilate the content of the original play for the sake of establishing some wholly new esthetic. It combats the assumptions of the classic with a series of new assumptions and forces it to bend under the power of a new polemic. And, of course, it doesn't always win. Sometimes the play's original ethic is so overpowering that an assault from an opposed viewpoint only confirms its original authority. In the course of these tussles, a certain number of theatrical effects will be produced, and an audience may be diverted by these effects—for their own sake— without realizing that, despite dazzling superficies, the play's original premise remains entirely intact. (In my view, this was the case with Peter Brook's *Midsummer Night's Dream* which decked out the play in an entirely new and unexpected wardrobe, but in no way altered its essential biology.) This is a traditional and entirely accept-able mode of Shakespearian interpretation: the Quick Flash method which disorients our visual expectations of what should be happening in a work of art but ultimately comforts us because we are shown that these 'differences' are still at the service of the original, and no matter how unorthadox the play's deportment, it remains inherently 'loyal' to Shakespeare. The experiments to which I would contrast this approach are brazen acts of treason and heinous acts of infidelity which shake to their very foundations the pillars of the original work. Such works

23

when they succeed are creations in their own right; ideological extensions of the work from which they sprang.

The question is not, as it is so often put, what is wrong with Shakespeare that we have to meddle with his works, but what is wrong with us that we are content to endure the diminishing returns of conventional dramatic reiteration; that we are prepared to go to the theatre and pretend that what dulls our minds and comforts our world-view is, by dint of such reassurances, culturally uplifting; not to realize that there is nothing so insidious as art that perpetuates the illusion that some kind of eternal truth is enshrined in a time-space continuum called 'a classic'; not to challenge the notion that its theatrical performance is *automatically* an experience because our presumption of a play's established worth guarantees us that experience. We all dupe ourselves in the theatre because we have been sold a bill of goods for a good quarter of a century before we enter. We get what we expect and we expect what we have been led to expect, and it is only when we don't get what we have been led to expect that we are on the threshold of having an experience. It is this cultural anticipation which swirls in our brains before the curtains rise on *Hamlet* or *Macbeth* or *Caesar* or *Lear,* which is the catalytic agent which makes it possible for theatregoers to 'have an experience'; to have it precisely because it is not the one they have been anticipating. We lose sight of the fact that, aesthetics notwithstanding, the theatre is primarily a social and psychological habit, and a great deal of what theatre artists prepare is based on the need to accommodate and feed that habit. Paradoxically, this is often done by persons asking themselves: how can we surprise our audiences, keep them from guessing what comes next, how can we give them 'something new'? The answers to these questions produce the pap of the boulevard theatre; the murder-mysteries, suspense-dramas, comedies and farces that suspend our disbeliefs only to fortify the age-old beliefs in whose name they have been only temporarily suspended. The same thinking also conditions the production of classics and so-called 'serious plays'. Even the 'Serious Artist' is primarily concerned with how

24

to distribute stale goods in dazzling new wrappers. It is only when the assumptions of art drastically change that a theatrical experience is possible. UBU ROI, in a sense, did that because it proceeded from a radical reconsideration of what a play could be and, fortunately, the audience's rejection of that idea fanned the flames of the new experience. In our time, *Waiting For Godot,* using an entirely negative aesthetic, did something like the same thing. It put a premium on what had always been taken to be an unquestioned liability: the absence of events, the non-happening. By so doing, it forced us to alter the readings on our cultural thermostat; to receive drama in a very different frame of mind and at a very different tempo. No new theatrical experience proceeds from the same assumptions as the last one. That is why there is nothing so lethal as 'trends' in art for, in standardizing what began life as an original impulse, it insults the integrity of the new experience by parodying it with reasonable facsimiles, thereby putting us further and further away from the possibility of yet another new experience. And, of course, our inability to distinguish artistic experiences from generally approved reasonable facsimiles is only a symptom of our lack of perception in life. How often is the myth of a party or a date or a romance escalated from the insensate reality on which it is based? If we could not idealize life, we could not bear it. And in the theatre, our idealizations are supported by art myths, education myths, media myths, innate desires for self delusion and the insatiable craving for magic. The theatre artist has all this to contend with. An audience is like the implacable face of a stopped clock that will resist all efforts to be wound to the correct time out of an obsessive desire to maintain the integrity of its broken mechanism. It is no wonder that art must occasionally give it a good shake to get it ticking again.

Charles Marowtiz
1975

The Shrew

For Thelma Holt
for making a silk purse out of a sow's ear

THE SHREW was first performed at The Hot Theatre, The Hague, Holland on October 18, 1973 with the following cast:

BIANCA (also THE GIRL)	Kay Barlow
KATHERINE	Thelma Holt
BAPTISTA	Jack Niles
HORTENSIO (also THE BOY)	Jeremy Nicholas
GRUMIO	Peter Davison
PETRUCHIO	Nikolas Simmonds

Directed by Charles Marowitz
Designed by Robin Don

A cry in the darkness. Lights up: BIANCA *tied to a pole, bound hand and foot.* KATE *holds the rope and slowly applies pressure by drawing it taut.*

BIANCA. Good sister, wrong me not nor wrong yourself
    To make a bondmaid and a slave of me.
    That I disdain. But for these other gawds,
    Unbind my hands, I'll pull them off myself,
    Yea, all my raiment, to my petticoat,
    Or what you command me will I do,
    So well I know my duty to my elders.

KATE. Of all thy suitors, here I charge thee, tell
    Whom thou lov'st best. See thou dissemble not.

BIANCA. Believe me, sister, of all the men alive
    I never yet beheld that special face
    Which I could fancy more than any other.

KATE. *(Pulls rope tighter)*
    Minion, thou liest. Is't not Hortensio?

BIANCA. If you affect him, sister, here I swear
    I'll plead for you myself but you shall have him.

KATE. O then, belike, you fancy riches more:
    You will have Grumio to keep you fair.

BIANCA. Is it for him you do envy me so?
    Nay, then you jest, and now I well perceive
    You have but jested with me all this while.
    I prithee, sister Kate, untie my hands.

KATE. If that be jest then all the rest was so.

    (Pulls rope tighter. BIANCA *screams.)*

(*Enter* BAPTISTA.)

BAPTISTA.   Why, how now, dame, whence grows this
   insolence?
Poor girl, she weeps. Bianca, stand aside.
For shame, thou hilding of a devilish spirit,
Why dost thou wrong her that did ne'er wrong thee?
When did she cross thee with a bitter word?

KATE.   Her silence flouts me and I'll be revenged.

BAPTISTA. What, in my sight? Bianca, get thee in.

(Taking BIANCA *round)*

Go ply thy needle; meddle not with her.

(BIANCA *exits crying.)*

KATE.   Nay, now I see
She is your treasure, she must have a husband;
I must dance barefoot on her wedding day,
And, for your love to her lead apes in hell.
Talk not to me; I will go sit and weep
Till I can find occasion of revenge.

(Exit.)

BAPTISTA.   *(Regards rope with which* BIANCA *was
tied)*

Was ever gentleman thus grieved as I?

(Lights out

Lights up.

PETRUCHIO *enters from left with* GRUMIO.
HORTENSIO *from right. All have the look and
manner of men involved in schemes and stratagems. A
certain unsentimental practicality is common to all.)*

HORTENSIO.   Petruchio.

PETRUCHIO.   My best beloved and approved friend.

HORTENSIO.   My old friend Grumio.
And tell me now, sweet friend, what happy gale
Blows you to Padua from old Verona?

PETRUCHIO.   Such wind as scatters young men through
   the world
  To seek their fortunes farther than at home,
  Where small experience grows. But in a few,
  Signior Hortensio, thus it stands with me:
  Antonio my father is deceased.

  (PETRUCHIO *pauses for a moment as if recalling
  his loss.* GRUMIO *sympathises;* HORTENSIO
  feels obliged to join in the mood then abruptly
  PETRUCHIO *shatters it with a mocking laugh
  which* GRUMIO *shares.* HORTENSIO, *suddenly
  the butt of the joke, is taken aback.*)

  Crowns in my purse I have and goods at home
  And so am come abroad to see the world.
  Happily to wive and thrive as best I may.

HORTENSIO.   Petruchio, shall I then come roundly to
   thee
  And wish thee to a shrewd ill-favoured wife?

PETRUCHIO.   Signior Hortensio, 'twixt such friends as
   we
  Few words suffice; and therefore if thou know
  One rich enough to be Petruchio's wife—
  As wealth is burthen of my wooing dance—
  Be she as foul as was Florentius' love,
  As old as Sibyl, and as curst and shrewd
  As Socrates' Xanthippe or a worse,
  She moves me not, or not removes, at least,
  Affection's edge in me, were she as rough
  As are the swelling Adriatic seas.
  I come to wive it wealthily in Padua;
  If wealthily, then happily in Padua.

HORTENSIO.   Thou'ldst thank me but a little for my
   counsel—
  And yet I'll promise thee she *shall* be rich,
  And very rich—
  Her house within the city
  Is richly furnished with plate and gold,
  Costly apparel, tents, and canopies,
  Fine lined, Turkey cushions bossed with pearl,

Pewter and brass, and all things that belong
To house or housekeeping.
Tis known her father hath no less
Then three argosies, besides two galliases
and twelve tight galleys . . .
But thou'rt too much my friend,
And I'll not wish thee to her.

(Moving off; stopped by GRUMIO)

GRUMIO. *(Close, threatening)* Nay, look you, sir, he
tells you flatly what his mind is. Why, give him
gold enough and marry him to a puppet or an
anglet-baby or an old trot with ne'er a tooth in
her head, though she has as many diseases as two-
and fifty horses. Why, nothing comes amiss so
money comes withal.

HORTENSIO. *(Reconsidering)*
I can, Petruchio, help thee to a wife
With wealth enough and young and beauteous,
Brought up as best becomes a gentlewoman.
Her only fault—and that is faults enough—
Is that she is intolerable curst
And shrewd and froward, so beyond all measure
That were my state far worser than it is,
I would not wed her for a mine of gold.

PETRUCHIO. Hortensio, peace. Thou know'st not
gold's effect.
And therefore let me be thus bold with you.
Tell me her father's name, and 'tis enough,
For I will board her though she chide as loud
As thunder when the clouds in Autumn crack.
I will not sleep Hortensio till I see her.

(PETRUCHIO *and* GRUMIO, *now threateningly
close to* HORTENSIO.)

HORTENSIO. Her father is Baptista Minola,
An affable and courteous gentleman.
Her name is Katherina Minola.

(PETRUCHIO *smiles at* GRUMO, *then at*
HORTENSIO, *who looks at him uncertainly.*

Black out.

Lights up.

32

BAPTISTA, *richly dressed, stands tentatively before* PETRUCHIO, HORTENSIO *and* GRUMIO.)

BAPTISTA. Good morrow, sirs.

PETRUCHIO. And you, good sir. Pray, have you not a daughter
Called Katherina, fair and virtuous?

BAPTISTA. I have a daughter, sir, called Katherina.

PETRUCHIO. *(Jovially, to* BAPTISTA)
I am a gentleman of Verona, sir,
That, hearing of her beauty and her wit,
Her affability and bashful modesty,
Her wondrous qualities and mild behaviour,
Am bold to show myself a forward guest
Within your house, to make mine eye the witness
Of that report which I so oft have heard.
And, for an entrance to my entertainment,
I do present you with a man of mine,

(Presenting HORTENSIO)

Cunning in music and the mathematics,
To instruct her fully in those sciences,
Whereof I knew she is not ignorant.
Accept of him, or else you do me wrong.
His name is . . . *(faltering)*

HORTENSIO. Litio, born in. . . *(faltering)*

PETRUCHIO. . . .Mantua!
And by good fortune I have lighted well
On this young man; for learning and behaviour
Fit for her turn, well read in poetry
And other books—good ones, I warrant ye.

BAPTISTA. Y'are welcome, sir, and they for your good sake.
But for my daughter Katherine, this I know,
She is not for your turn the more my grief.

(A threatening silence ensues. Gradually,
BAPTISTA *becomes aware of it, and turns to find a grim, dead-eyed* PETRUCHIO, *who begins to speak slowly and menacingly.)*

PETRUCHIO. I see you do not mean to part with her,
Or else you like not of my company.

BAPTISTA.   Mistake me not; I speak but as I find.
　　　Whence are you, sir? What may I call your name?

PETRUCHIO.   Petruchio is my name, Antonio's son,
　　　A man well known throughout all Italy.

BAPTISTA.   I . . . know him well. You are welcome for
　　　his sake.

(PETRUCHIO *suddenly restores an air of bonhomie.*
HORTENSIO *and* GRUMIO *place* BAPTISTA *on
a stool alongside* PETRUCHIO *then gather round
the two men—rather too closely to* BAPTISTA.)

PETRUCHIO.   Signior Baptista, my business asketh
　　　haste,
　　　And every day I cannot come to woo.
　　　You knew my father, and in him me,
　　　Left solely heir to all his lands and goods,
　　　Which I have bettered rather then decreased.
　　　Then tell me, if I get your daughter's love
　　　What dowry shall I have with her to wife?

BAPTISTA.   After my death the one half of my lands,

(PETRUCHIO *looks to* HORTENSIO *to see if this
is enough.* HORTENSIO *casually rubs a finger
against his nose. In the pause,* BAPTISTA *decides
to up the ante.)*

And in possession twenty thousand crowns.

PETRUCHIO.   And, for that dowry, I'll assure her of
　　　Her widowhood, be it that she survive me,
　　　In all my lands and leases whatsoever.
　　　Let specialities be therefore drawn between us
　　　That convenants may be kept on either hand.

BAPTISTA.   Ay, when the special thing is well obtained,
　　　That is, her love, for that is all in all.

PETRUCHIO.   Why, that is nothing, for I tell you,
　　　father,
　　　I am as peremptory as she proud-minded.
　　　And where two raging fires meet together
　　　They do consume the thing that feeds their fury.
　　　Though little fire grows great with little wind,
　　　Yet extreme gusts will blow out fire and all.
　　　So I to her, and so she yields to me,
　　　For I am rough and woo not like a babe.

BAPTISTA.   Well mayst thou woo, and happy to be thy
          speed!
     But be thou armed for some unhappy words.

PETRUCHIO.   Ay, to the proof, as mountains are for
          winds
     That shake not, though they blow perpetually.

BAPTISTA.   *(Coolly, under-cutting* PETRUCHIO's
     rhetoric)
     Signior Petruchio, will you go with us
     Or shall I send my daughter Kate to you?

PETRUCHIO.   I pray you do. I'll attend her here
     And woo her with some spirit when she comes.

     (BAPTISTA *exits.*

     *The three men laugh together, feeling they have
     successfully jumped the first hurdle; then, as if
     taking* PETRUCHIO *through his catechisms,*
     HORTENSIO *and* GRUMIO *begin to fire questions
     at him—clearly testing his grasp of previously learnt
     information.)*

HORTENSIO.   Say that she rail?

PETRUCHIO.   Why then I'll tell her plain
     She sings as sweetly as a nightingale.

GRUMIO.   Say that she frown?

PETRUCHIO.   I'll say she looks as clear
     As morning roses nearly washed with dew.

HORTENSIO.   Say she be mute and will not speak a
          word?

PETRUCHIO.   Then I'll command her volubility
     And say she uttereth piercing eloquence.

GRUMIO.   If she do bid thee pack?

PETRUCHIO.   *(Momentarily stumped, consults
     rolled-up piece of paper in his boot)*
     I'll give her thanks
     As though she bid me stay by her a week.

HORTENSIO.   If she deny to wed?

PETRUCHIO.   I'll crave the day
     When I shall ask the bans and when be married.

35

But here she comes . . .

(HORTENSIO *and* GRUMIO *exit quickly.*)

. . . and now, Petruchio, speak.

(KATE *enters; very regal, very composed.*
PETRUCHIO *is in a self-induced state of contemplation.* KATE *waits for him to acknowledge her; as he does not do so, she begins to leave.*

After a step or two, PETRUCHIO *turns and begins.*)

PETRUCHIO.   *(Brightly)* Good morrow, Kate, for that's
    your name, I hear.

KATE.   Well have you heard, but something hard of
        hearing.
    They call me Katherine that do talk of me.

PETRUCHIO.   *(Insolently)* You lie, in faith, for you are
        called plain Kate,
    And bonny Kate, and sometimes Kate the curst.
    But *(bright)* Kate, the prettiest Kate in Christendom,
    Kate of Kate Hall, my super-dainty Kate,
    For dainties are all Kates, and therefore, Kate,
    Take this of me, Kate of my consolation.
    Hearing thy mildness praised in every town,
    Thy virtues spoke of, and thy beauty sounded—
    Yet not so deeply as to thee belongs—
    Myself am moved to woo thee for my wife.

KATE.   Moved! In good time, let him that moved you
        hither
    Remove you hence. I knew you at the first
    You were a movable.

PETRUCHIO.   Why, what's a movable?

KATE.   A joint stool.

PETRUCHIO.   *(Sitting, jovial)*
    Thou hast hit it; come sit on me.

KATE.   *(Clever)*
    Asses are made to bear and so are you.

PETRUCHIO.   *(Hard, offensive)*
    Women are made to bear and so are you.

KATE.   No such jade as you, if me you mean.

PETRUCHIO.   *(Lightening)*
    Alas, good Kate, I will not burden thee,

For, knowing thee to be but young and light—

KATE.   Too light for such a swain as you to catch
And yet as heavy as my weight should be.

PETRUCHIO.   Come, come, you wasp, i' faith you are
too angry.

KATE.   If I be waspish, best beware my sting.

PETRUCHIO.   My remedy is then to pluck it out.

KATE.   Ay, if the fool could find it where it lies.

PETRUCHIO.   Who knows not where a wasp does wear
his sting?

(Vulgarly) In his tail.

KATE.   In his tongue.

PETRUCHIO.   Whose tongue?

KATE.   Yours if you talk of tales and so farewell.

PETRUCHIO.   What, with my tongue in your tail? Nay,
come again.
Good Kate, I am a gentleman—

KATE.   That I'll try. *(She strikes him.)*

(The slap dissolves all banter. PETRUCHIO *looks*
KATE *coldly in the eye and begins to speak
quietly, in dead earnest.)*

PETRUCHIO.   I swear I'll cuff you if you strike again.

KATE.   *(Wary)* So may you lose your arms: If you strike
me you are no gentleman,
And if no gentleman, why then no arms.

PETRUCHIO.   *(Makes enormous effort to banish his
emnity and impose gaiety; kneeling)*
A herald, Kate? O, put me in thy books.

KATE.   What is your crest? A coxcomb?

PETRUCHIO.   *(Making a straight pass)*
A combless cock, so Kate will be my hen.

KATE.   No cock of mine; you crow too like a craven.

PETRUCHIO.   Nay, come, Kate, come, you must not
look so sour.

37

KATE. It is my fashion when I see a crab.

PETRUCHIO. *(Finding it difficult to play the game)*
Why, here's no crab, and therefore look not
sour.

KATE. There is, there is.

PETRUCHIO. Then show it me.

KATE. Had I a glass I would.

PETRUCHIO. *(Slowly, menacingly, first threat of
physical violence)*
What, you mean my face?

KATE. Well aimed of such a young one.

PETRUCHIO. *(Inspecting her hair-line)* Now, by Saint
George, I am too young for you.

KATE. Yet you are withered.

PETRUCHIO. 'Tis with cares.

KATE. I care not. *(Starts to go)*

PETRUCHIO. Nay, hear you, Kate, in sooth you scape
not so. *(Blocking her way)*

KATE. I chafe you if I tarry. Let me go.

PETRUCHIO. No, not a whit.

*(There is a pause during which KATE assesses her
situation. Since her path is barred she resolutely
decides to remain; turns and sits.)*

I find you passing gentle.
'Twas told me you were rough and coy and sullen,
And now I find report a very liar,
For thou art pleasant, gamesome, passing courteous,
But slow in speech, yet sweet as springtime
            flowers.
Thou canst not frown, thou canst not look
            askance,
Nor bite the lip as angry wenches will,
Nor hast thou pleasure to be cross in talk,
But thou with mildness entertain'st thy wooers,
With gentle conference, soft and affable
Why does the world report that Kate doth limp?
O sland'rous world! Kate like the hazel-twig

38

Is straight and slender, and as brown in hue
As hazelnuts and sweeter than the kernels.
O, let me see thee walk. Thou does not halt.

KATE. Go, fool and whom thou keep'st command.

PETRUCHIO. *(Falsely cynical)*
Did ever Dian so become a grove
As Kate this chamber with her princely gait?
O, be thou Dian and let her be Kate,
And then let Kate be chaste and Dian sportful!

KATE. Where did you study all this goodly speech?

PETRUCHIO. It is extempore, from my mother-wit.

KATE. A witty mother! Witless else her son.

PETRUCHIO. Am I not wise?

KATE. Yes, keep you warm. *(Starts to go)*

PETRUCHIO. Marry, so I mean, sweet Katherine, in
thy bed.

(PETRUCHIO *grabs* KATE's *crotch. She is
momentarily stunned by the suddenness of this
brutish move. Slowly* PETRUCHIO *takes firm
hold of her wrists. There is visible pressure.)*

And therefore, setting all this chat aside,
Thus in plain terms: your father hath consented
That you shall be my wife, your dowry 'greed on,
And will you, nill you, I will marry you.

(Enter BAPTISTA, HORTENSIO, GRUMIO)

For I am he am born to tame you, Kate,
And bring you from a wild Kate to a Kate
Conformable as other household Kates.
Here comes your father. Never make denial.
I must and will have Katherine to my wife.

BAPTISTA. Now, Signior Petruchio, how speed you
with my daughter?

PETRUCHIO. *(Suddenly jovial; eyes telling another
story to* KATE)
How but well, sir? How but well?
It were impossible I should speed amiss.

BAPTISTA. Why, how now, daughter Katherine, in

your dumps?

KATE.   Call you me daughter? Now, I promise you
    You have showed a tender fatherly regard
    To wish me wed to one half lunatic,
    A madcap ruffian and a swearing Jack
    That thinks with oaths to face the matter out.

PETRUCHIO.   Father, 'tis thus: yourself and all the
        world
    That talked of her have talked amiss of her.
    If she be curst it is for policy,
    For she's not froward but modest as the dove.
    She is not hot but temperate as the morn;
    For patience she will prove a second Grissel
    And Roman Lucrece for her chastity.
    And to conclude, we have 'greed so well together
    That upon Sunday is the wedding day.

KATE.   I'll see thee hanged on Sunday first.

PETRUCHIO.   *(Taking* BAPTISTA *round; playing
    down* KATE's *visible opposition to the match)*
    I tell you, 'tis incredible to believe
    How much she loves me. O, the kindest Kate,
    She hung about my neck, and kiss on kiss
    She vied so fast, protesting oath on oath,
    That in a twink she won me to her love.
    O, you are novices. 'Tis a world to see
    How tame, when men and women are alone,
    A meacock wretch can make the curstest shrew.
    Give me thy hand, Kate.

    (Holds out hand.)

    GRUMIO, *who has worked his way round to*
    KATE's *side, forcibly takes her hand and plants it
    into* PETRUCHIO's.*)*

    I will unto Venice
    To buy apparel 'gainst the wedding day.
    Provide the feast, father, and bid the guests;
    I will be sure my Katherine shall be fine.

    (Hand out to BAPTISTA*)*

BAPTISTA.   I know not what to say.

    (HORTENSIO, *who has worked his way round to*
    BAPTISTA's *side, takes his hand and clamps it into*

PETRUCHIO's.)

God send you joy, Petruchio! 'Tis a match.

HORTENSIO and GRUMIO.   Amen, say we.

PETRUCHIO.   Father, and wife, and gentlemen, adieu.
I will to Venice; Sunday comes apace.
We will have rings and things and fine array,
And kiss me Kate; we will be married 'a Sunday.

(PETRUCHIO *moves to kiss* KATE. *She draws
back instinctively.* GRUMIO *takes hold of her
arms which prevents her from moving any further
back.* PETRUCHIO *moves forward, takes* KATE's
*face in his hands. She goes limp and lifeless as he
firmly plants a kiss on her mouth. When he removes
his lips,* KATE's *barely perceptible smile suggests
that although he can take things by force, he will
never get her wilfully to yield.*

PETRUCHIO *receives* KATE's *look, sensing the
hollowness of his victory.*

Fade out.)

GIRL (BIANCA *now dressed contemporary*) *strolls out from centre-doorway. She is smoking a cigeratte. Stands looking off. In a moment,* BOY (HORTENSIO *now dressed in modern clothes) appears at doorway;* GIRL *turns her head to register his appearance then turns again and smokes. Gradually, the* BOY *moves in.*

HE.   You knew I was watching you in there, didn't you?

SHE.   *(Aloof)* Were you?

HE.   Didn't you feel it?

SHE.   Not really.

HE.   I thought you did.

SHE.   Perhaps.

HE.   That's a very elusive reply.

SHE.   Elusive?

HE.   You're not very easy to pin down.

SHE.   Do you want to?

HE.   It's an idea.

   (Pause. SHE *smokes.* HE *looks for a ploy.)*

   It's bloody boring in there, isn't it?

SHE.   It always is.

HE.   Why do you go?

SHE.   I don't know. I always expect it to improve.

HE.   You're an optimist.

SHE.   Why did you come?

HE: *(Suddenly improvising)* My astrology-chart said something big was in store for me. 'Expect something strong and fiery to happen that will last a long time.'

SHE.   It could be heartburn.

HE.   *(Hyping)* Where's your romanticism, your sense of mystery. Don't you believe it's all written in the stars?

42

SHE.   Do you?

HE.   Yes, but in very small print. And I'm not even sure it's in English.

SHE.   Doesn't seem worth all the trouble then, does it?

HE.   Not if you're not a romantic.

SHE.   And you are.

HE.   President of the Club.

SHE.   Very large membership?

HE.   Enormous, and lots of celebrities as well. Wasn't it Oscar Wilde, one of our fully paid-up members by the way, who said, I may be lying in the gutter but I'm looking at the stars.

SHE.   *Was* he lying in the gutter?

HE.   No, I expect he was in a posh Mayfair club with objets d'art on every side and a five-course dinner on the boil. What a charlatan!

SHE.   Exactly.

HE.   *(Losing the thread)* What do you mean, exactly?

(SHE smiles at him, continues to smoke, and moves a little further off.

After a moment, HE takes her hand and begins to study it. This goes on for a while.)

SHE.   Do you read palms as well?

HE.   Oh yes, and Tarot cards, tea leaves, bumps-on-the-head and, on a good day, even cigarette ash. *(Continues to study hand)*

SHE.   Do I pass inspection?

HE.   *(Close)* Flying colours.

(They look at each other. SHE touches his cheek. HE makes a move toward her for the embrace. She breaks and walks away casually.)

HE.   *(After registering the rebuff)* What do you do?

SHE.   As I like. Usually.

HE.   Are you doing what you like at the moment?

SHE.   At this very moment?

HE.   Yes.

SHE.   I think so.

HE.   And what's that?

SHE.   Not very much of anything in particular.

HE.   *(Mock-offended)* Is that really the way you'd describe our conversation?

SHE.   It's how I'd describe yours.

HE.   I think that's what the social psychologists call 'holding your own'.

SHE.   I never read them.

HE.   *You* don't have to.

(Pause)

SHE.   And you? Are you doing as you like?

HE.   *(A motto)* I never do as I like. I always do as I must.

SHE.   How dreary for you.

HE.   Not at all. It's very good for the soul to 'do as one must'. It develops all kinds of traits like discipline, pride, shrewdness, self-sufficiency . . .

SHE.   Egotism?

HE.   *(Caught)* That's a by-product, I suppose.

SHE.   In rather plentiful supply.

HE.   *(Mask away)* Well, I have to impress you with something. Language is all I have.

SHE.   And even that's somewhat impoverished.

(Pause.)

HE.   *(At a loss; tries a new tack)* You know, when you're watching someone for something like two hours across a crowded room, you tend to make up little stories about them. I've got quite a file of stuff about you.

SHE. Really?

HE. Born in Surrey—or possibly Hampshire. Father hunts and shoots, dabbles in real estate, wears plus fours. Sent you through boarding school, a year on the continent and then Girton, finishing with a bevy of firsts in lots of esoteric subjects like medieval epistemology or 12th century ceramics. Flat in Kensington, credit account in Dickens and Jones, and a supercharged Fiat all of your very own. Am I getting warm?

SHE. You're not even tepid.

HE. I should think the main difference between us is purely economic.

SHE. Do you mean money?

HE. Yes.

SHE. Why don't you say so. 'Economic' is a kind of camouflage-word, isn't it.

HE. 'Money' is so crude.

SHE. Only if you haven't got any.

HE. Touché.

SHE. Were we fencing?

HE. I thought I felt a little nick.

SHE. I'm sorry.

HE. Oh, I don't mind.

SHE. Good. Then I don't have to apologize.

(Pause. HE approaches her, touches her hair, gradually kisses her. SHE yields in the kiss then, as his kiss becomes more familiar, breaks.)

SHE. *(Holding him slightly off. Quietly)* Do you expect sex as a matter of course?

HE. *(Surprised)* Were we talking about sex?

SHE. Weren't you?

HE. *(Admitting it)* I suppose I was.

SHE. Do you?

45

HE. As a matter of course. No. Of course not. It never is a matter of course.

SHE. It isn't with me. I thought it would be fairer to let you know.

HE. *(Dryly)* Thanks.

SHE. You're welcome. (SHE *kisses him hard.* HE *reels slightly recovering from the clinch)* You're very nice. Even if you are a bit of a clot. *(Moves away)*

HE. I suppose I had better take that as a compliment.

SHE. The one thing that all men have in common is the ability to produce great billowing waves of boredom. Lately, one way and another, I seem to have got quite drenched.

HE. Now, women are never boring. Being beautiful, they never risk boredom by ever using their minds.

SHE. But not all women are beautiful. Some are quite plain.

HE. *(Off-hand)* Yes, those are the boring ones.

SHE. Doesn't beauty ever get boring?

HE. Never.

SHE. Not even years afterward—twenty, thirty years afterward?

HE. Not if it's *real* beauty.

SHE. Real beauty, as you call it, has the alarming tendency to turn into *real* old age, and there's nothing beautiful about that.

HE. But why should you be worrying about that, being as beautiful as you are.

SHE. *(Regards him wryly for a moment)* You get to the pictures quite a bit, don't you?

HE. *(Assuming the ice is now broken; levelling)* I watched you all night long in there. Staring like a bloody owl. Don't tell me you didn't notice.

SHE. I'm not sure.

HE. You don't kiss like you're not sure.

46

SHE.   Are you sure you're not jumping to conclusions?

HE.   Do you think I am?

SHE.   I think . . . *(Suddenly playing the grand lady)* you're a very forward youth.

HE.   *(Playing the game, curtsies)* Your humble servant, m'lady.

SHE.   You may kiss my foot.

(In character, HE *does so.* SHE *then extends hand, he kisses that. She extends finger, he kisses that.)*

That will do, thank you.

HE.   Thank you, m'lady. Much obliged, m'lady. *(Jumps up)* Look, I've got a 1964 Austin outside and a back-and-doubles route to Paddington where a bottle of vintage bubbly is cooling in the fridge. *(Displays keys)* How say you?

SHE.   *(Remote, but not aggressive)* I've got to be going.

HE.   What?

(SHE *goes.)*

Why? Look, can I ring you? Can I have your number?

SHE.   *(At doorway)* I'm sorry. I have to make a very early start in the morning.

(SHE *leaves.* HE *stands flustered facing doorway.*

Black out.)

A bell tolls grimly in the distance.

Lights up on KATE, *standing motionless like a doll, wearing a simple white shift; eyes straight ahead; a vague sense of being the victim of some grim, unwanted social ceremony.*

Upstage right of her stands BIANCA *holding bridal veil. Upstage left,* GRUMIO. *Downstage left,* BAPTISTA, *supervising the ceremony. As the bell tolls mournfully,* HORTENSIO *slowly comes forward holding* KATE'*s bridal gown open before him. He stops in front of her;* GRUMIO *steps behind her;* KATE'*s arms are lifted straight out as if they were those of a mechanical doll. Together* HORTENSIO *and* GRUMIO *slip her into the bridal gown. When this is done,* BIANCA *comes forward and places the bridal veil over* KATE'*s head. All four then regard her from their respective corners.* KATE *turns her head to* BAPTISTA *who nods his approval. The bell stops tolling, full lights come up and the formality of the previous scene suddenly evaporates.* BIANCA *and* GRUMIO *exit.* BAPTISTA *crosses angrily downstage and* KATE, *irritably upstage.*

BAPTISTA. *(To* GRUMIO) This is the 'pointed day
    That Katherine and Petruchio should be married,
    And yet we hear not of our son-in-law.
    What will be said? What mockery will it be
    To want the bridegroom when the priest attends
    To speak the ceremonial rites of marriage!
    What says Litio to this shame of ours?

KATE. No shame but mine. I must, forsooth, be forced
    To give my hand opposed against my heart
    Unto a mad-brain rudesby, full of spleen,
    Who wooed in haste and means to wed at leisure.
    I told you, I, he was a frantic fool,
    Hiding his bitter jests in blunt behaviour.
    And to be noted for a merry man,
    He'll woo a thousand, 'point the day of marriage,
    Make friends, invite, and proclaim the banns,
    Yet never means to wed where he hath wooed.

HORTENSIO. Patience, good Katherine, and Baptista
      too.
    Upon my life, Petruchio means but well,
    Whatever fortune stays him from his word
    Though he be blunt, I know him passing wise;

Though he be merry, yet withal he's honest.

KATE.   Would Katherine had never seen him though!

(Exit)

GRUMIO. *(Entering, pretending shock)*
Why, Petruchio is coming.

(PETRUCHIO *enters dressed in a sumptuous female*
bridal gown, similar to KATE's. *No female wig; no hat;*
masculine head on female form.)

PETRUCHIO.   Come, where be these gallants? Who's at
home?

BAPTISTA.   You are welcome, sir.

PETRUCHIO.   And yet I come not well.

GRUMIO.   And yet you halt not.

BAPTISTA.   Not so well appareled
As I wish you were.

PETRUCHIO.   But where is Kate? Where is my lovely
bride?
Gentles, methinks you frown.
And wherefore gaze this goodly company
As if they saw some wondrous monument,
Some comet or unusual prodigy?
How does my father?

BAPTISTA.   Why, sir, you know this is your wedding
day
First were we sad, fearing you would not come,
Now sadder that you come so unprovided.
Fie, doff this habit, shame to your estate,
An eyesore to our solemn festival.

GRUMIO. *(Faking outrage)*
And tell us what occasion of import
Hath all so long detained you from your wife
And sent you hither so unlike yourself.

PETRUCHIO.   Tedious it were to tell and harsh to hear.
Sufficeth, I am come to keep my word
But where is Kate? I stay too long from her.
The morning wears, 'tis time we were at church.

HORTENSIO. *(Faking outrage)* See not your bride in
these unreverent robes.

GRUMIO.   Go to my chamber; put on clothes of mine.

PETRUCHIO.   Not I, believe me; thus I'll visit her.

BAPTISTA.   But thus, I trust, you will not marry her.

PETRUCHIO.   *(Sudden outburst)*
    Good sooth, even thus; therefore ha' done with
        words.
    To me she's married, not unto my clothes.
    But what a fool am I to chat with you
    When I should bid good morrow to my bride
    And seal the title with a lovely kiss.

    (KATE *re-enters followed by bridesmaid—*
    BIANCA. *She stops as she sees* PETRUCHIO *in*
    dress. All stand anticipating her reaction.
    PETRUCHIO *slowly turns and confronts* KATE.
    Then, making no attempt to conceal the male
    within the female attire, walks very slowly
    towards KATE. *When he arrives before her, he*
    suddenly performs an unexpected female curtsey,
    abruptly defuses the charged atmosphere and
    places himself beside his bride.)

PETRUCHIO.   Gentlemen and friends, I thank you
        for your pains.
    I know you think to dine with me today
    And have prepared great store of wedding cheer,
    But so it is, my haste doth call me hence
    And therefore here I mean to take my leave.

BAPTISTA.   Is't possible you will away tonight?

PETRUCHIO.   I must away today, before night come.
    Make it no wonder; if you knew my business,
    You would entreat me rather go than stay.
    And, honest company, I thank you all
    That have beheld me give away myself
    To this most patient, sweet, and virtuous wife.
    Dine with my father, drink a health to me,
    For I must hence, and farewell to you all.

    (Shakes hands with HORTENSIO, GRUMIO,
    BAPTISTA *and begins to move off.)*

GRUMIO.   Let us entreat you stay till after dinner.

PETRUCHIO.   It may not be.

HORTENSIO.   Let me entreat you.

PETRUCHIO.   It cannot be.

KATE.   Let me entreat you.

(PETRUCHIO *still facing away, halts.*)

PETRUCHIO.   I am content.

KATE.   Are you content to stay?

PETRUCHIO.   *(Turning to* KATE)
I am content you shall entreat me stay,
But yet not stay, entreat me how you can.

KATE.   Now if you love me, stay.

(PETRUCHIO *approaches* KATE *slowly and,
when close, pretends to call to* GRUMIO *for
horse—although the double-entendre insult to*
KATE *is registered by all.*)

PETRUCHIO.   My horse!

KATE.   *(Fiery-hot)* Nay, then
Do what thou canst, I will not go today,
No, nor tomorrow, not till I please myself.
The door is open, sir, there lies your way.
You may be jogging whilst your boots are green;
For me, I'll not be gone till I please myself.

PETRUCHIO.   O Kate, content thee; prithee, be not
angry.

KATE.   I will be angry. What hast thou to do?
Father, be quiet; he shall stay my leisure.
Gentlemen, forward to the bridal dinner.
I see a woman may be made a fool
If she had not a spirit to resist.

PETRUCHIO.   They shall go forward, Kate, at thy
command.
Obey the bride, you that attend on her.
Go to the feast, revel and domineer,
Carouse full measure to her maidenhead,
Be mad and marry, or go hang yourselves.
But for my bonny Kate, she must with me.
I will be master of what is mine own.

(During the following speech, PETRUCHIO *slowly strips off bridal gown, revealing his male attire underneath.)*

She is my goods, my chattels; she is my house,
My household stuff, my field, my barn,
My horse, my ox, my ass, my anything,
And here she stands. Touch her whoever dare,
I'll bring mine action on the proudest he
That stops my way in Padua.

(PETRUCHIO *grabs* KATE's *arm and starts to usher her out. She manages a momentary halt at the doorway during which she glowers at a helpless* BAPTISTA *and then is briskly removed.*

BAPTISTA *makes an instinctive move towards the doorway to come to* KATE's *aid but* GRUMIO *steps down to bar his path.* BAPTISTA *thinks better of it and moves to* BIANCA. *She turns away from him coldly. Visibly drenched with guilt and uncertain,* BAPTISTA *moves to opposite exit and out.* GRUMIO *turns upstage and looks to where* KATE *and* PETRUCHIO *have exited.* HORTENSIO *steps down and coolly addresses* BIANCA.)

HORTENSIO.   Mistress, what's your opinion of your sister?

BIANCA.   *(Grimly, but secretly pleased)*

That being mad herself, she is madly mated.

(An inscrutable look to HORTENSIO.

Black out.)

Lights up. The BOY *and* GIRL *confronting each other.*

HE. Were you just trying it on?

SHE. Trying what on?

HE. Come on, don't play games.

SHE. I don't know what you're on about.

HE. You were cooped up with that guy for almost three hours. I might just as well have been the hatstand.

SHE. Oh for God's sake. You're not going to get up tight because of that.

HE. How would you like to hang around at a party for over three hours, drinking lousy wine, and making small talk while the person you're supposed to be with is snuggling in some remote corner of the room. That's your idea of companionship, is it?

SHE. We weren't snuggling—we were discussing. You make it sound as if he was having me on the carpet.

HE. He might just as well have done.

SHE. Oh come on. . . we're both out of kindergarten.

HE. That's not the point.

SHE. Well it escapes me.

HE. Lots of things seem to escape you these days.

SHE. Look. The boy had read a book I'd just finished. He had opinions about it. They were interesting, different from mine, and we just discussed it. Now since when did that become a capital offense?

HE. And my line of conversation is just too dreary to bother about.

SHE. We're always conversing. You don't go to a party to pick up the threads of pillow talk from the night before, do you? I thought you seemed quite interested in that bleached blonde. How did I know you were suffering?

HE. She wasn't bleached and I wasn't suffering. If a guy brings a girl to a party, there's usually some kind of vague understanding that they're together.

SHE. Thanks for the tip. Next time I'll wear a sign: 'Property of. . .'

HE. I don't mean that.

SHE. I know exactly what you mean. It's just that grotty old background exerting its traditional pull, isn't it? 'She's mine. I'm hers.' Public, neon-lit togetherness.

HE. You make it sound like some horrible crime to want to be with the girl you're engaged to.

SHE. Not a horrible crime—just a niggling little lapse of taste.

HE. Are we engaged or aren't we?

SHE. Yes, I suppose we are.

HE. That's not the kind of thing that's usually up in the air. Either we are or we aren't.

SHE. We are, but I don't like to make a public issue out of it.

HE. What's that supposed to mean?

SHE. I mean 'engaged' 'betrothed' 'spoken for'. . . they're words that make me wriggle inside. Like being stamped with a branding-iron.

HE. You mean we're not engaged.

SHE. We're in love, isn't that enough?

HE. People in love usually get engaged.

SHE. All right, we're engaged.

HE. *(Exasperated)* I don't know where I am with you.

SHE. *(Goes to him; a peace-making move)* Don't let's quarrel about something as silly as this.

HE. *(In her arms)* If I didn't love you, I wouldn't give two hoots who you were holed up in a corner with; don't you see that?

SHE. I do. You're really sweet.

HE. *(Breaking away)* Now I feel like I'm being bribed with candy.

SHE. *(Irritable)* Nothing seems to satisfy you tonight.

HE. *(Hot)* Are you trying to tell me you were only fascinated by that guy's brains.

SHE. No, I was helplessly infatuated with his physique. In between quotations from Freud and Adler, he told me he had a camel parked outside and invited me to spend the rest of my life as a slave in his harem.

HE. Very funny.

SHE. Not as funny as the look on your face.

HE. The way I was brought up, if you loved someone, you thought of spending at least part of your life with her.

SHE. *(Wearying)* It's a little late for nostalgia about 'the good old days' and the 'little old shack by the railway track'.

HE. Everytime I bring up the subject you just shy away. I mean are we or aren't we? Are we together or just. . .

SHE. If you say 'ships passing in the night' I'll scream.

HE. You don't want to be tied down. Admit it.

SHE. Does anyone? I mean besides heiffers and bondage-pervs?

HE. What the hell are we doing with each other?

SHE. *(Taking him round)* Why do you keep demanding answers all the time?

HE. Because I'm bothered by questions. You don't seem to be bothered by anything.

SHE. I'm bothered by seeing you tied up in knots like this. Look, I'm sorry if I offended you tonight. I didn't mean to. I got involved in a conversation that interested me, and, well, I suppose I neglected you. I'm sorry about that. Really.

HE. *(Contrite, back in her arms)* I'm just being a grouch—as usual.

SHE. *(Baby-talking)* Big bad grouch.

HE.   I heard little flashes of all that hyper-intellectual stuff all night, and I suppose I just got angry because I was, well, barred.

SHE.   We have much more interesting things to do.

HE.   I'm just being a clot.

SHE.   Big grouchy clot. *(They kiss; then remain in each other's arms.)*

HE.   *(Quietly)* Can you stay tonight?

SHE.   I've got to be at dad's in the morning.

HE.   I can run you back. Before work.

SHE.   Do you think you'll have the energy.

HE.   That's up to you.

SHE.   Then I doubt it.

HE.   I'm sorry about all that stupid stuff. . .

SHE.   Shh. . .*(Kisses him quiet.)*

HE.   I was just being. . .

SHE.   A clot. I know. *(Kisses him.)*

HE.   Is everything okay?

SHE.   *(Taking his hand)* Come on.

(Fade out.)

Lights up.

PETRUCHIO's *house. Very dark. Very Gothic. Sparse wooden table. Three stools.*

PETRUCHIO's *voice is heard offstage.*

PETRUCHIO.   Where be these knaves?

> (PETRUCHIO, *dusty from his travels, enters;* KATE *behind.)*

> What, no man at door
> To hold my stirrup nor to take my horse?
> Where is Nathaniel, Gregory, Philip?
> What, no attendance? No regard? No duty?
> Where is the foolish knave I sent before?

GRUMIO.   *(Wearing mask of gnarled brutish servant)*
Here, sir, as foolish as I was before.

PETRUCHIO.   You peasant swain! You whoreson
        malt-horse drudge!
Go, rascal, go and fetch my supper in.

> *(Exit* GRUMIO.)

> Sit down, Kate, and welcome.

> (PETRUCHIO *sits at head of table awaiting service. A long pause during which his irritation grows then erupts suddenly and pounds table.)*

> Food, Food, FOOD!!!

> (HORTENSIO, *also wearing ugly, gnarled servant's mask, enters.)*

> Why, when, I say?—Nay, good sweet Kate, sit down.
> Off with my boots, you rogue, you villain!

> (HORTENSIO *goes to remove* PETRUCHIO's *boot.)*

> *(Sings)*'It was the friar of orders gray,
> As he forth walked on his way'—
> Out, you rogue, you pluck my foot awry!

> (PETRUCHIO *kicks* HORTENSIO *and sends him sprawling. Eventually exits.)*

> Be merry, Kate. Some water here! What ho!

(Suddenly aware of absence, looking about furtively)

Where are my slippers? Shall I have some water?

(HORTENSIO re-enters with bowl.)

Come, Kate, and wash, and welcome heartily.

(HORTENSIO drops bowl.)

You whoreson villain, will you let it fall?

(PETRUCHIO twists HORTENSIO's arm behind his back visibly inflicting severe pain.)

KATE.   Patience, I pray you. 'Twas a fault unwilling.

PETRUCHIO.   A whoreson, beetle-headed, flap-eared knave!

GRUMIO.   *(Off)* The tailor now stays thy leisure.

(GRUMIO, now dressed as tailor and without servant's mask, enters carrying garments. HORTENSIO scampers out.)

PETRUCHIO.   Come, tailor, let us see these ornaments. What news with you, sir?

GRUMIO.   Here is the cap your worship did bespeak.

PETRUCHIO.   *(Taking the hat in his hand and examining it; slowly developing dissatisfaction)*
Why, this was molded on a porringer—
A velvet dish. Fie, fie, 'tis lewd and filthy.
Why, 'tis a cockle or a walnut shell,
A knack, a toy, a trick, a baby's cap.
Away with it. *(Tosses hat aside)* Come, let me have
    bigger.

KATE.   *(Picking up hat)* I'll have no bigger.
This doth fit the time,
And gentlewomen wear such caps as these.

PETRUCHIO.   When you are gentle you shall have one
    too
And not till then.

KATE.   *(Suddenly brazen)*
Why, sir, I trust I may have leave to speak,
And speak I will. I am no child, no babe.
Your betters have endured me say my mind,
And if you cannot, best you stop your ears.

My tongue will tell the anger of my heart,
Or else my heart, concealing it, will break,
And rather than it shall I will be free
Even to the uttermost, as I please, in words.

PETRUCHIO.   Why, thou sayest true. It is a paltry cap,
I love thee well in that thou lik'st it not.

KATE.   Love me or love me not, I like the cap,
And it I will have or I will have none.

PETRUCHIO.   *(Tearing hat in two)*
Thy gown? Why, aye. Come, let us see't.

(Examining the dress; slowly turning critical)

O mercy, God! What masking stuff is here?
What's this? A sleeve? Tis like a demi-cannon.
What, up and down, carved like an apple-tart?
Why, what, a devil's name tailor, call'st thou this?

GRUMIO.   You bid me make it orderly and well,
According to the fashion and the time.

PETRUCHIO.   I did not bid you mar it to the time.
Go, hop me over every kennel home,
For you shall hop without my custom.
I'll none of it. Hence, make your best of it.
(Throws dress down)

KATE.   *(Picks up dress)*
I never saw a better-fashioned gown.
More quaint, more pleasing, nor more commend-
      able.
Belike you mean to make a puppet of me.

PETRUCHIO.   *(Suddenly aware of the tailor's diabolical
purpose, turns on him threateningly)*
Why true, he means to make a puppet of thee.

GRUMIO.   *(Cowering at* PETRUCHIO's *approach)*
She says your worship means to make a puppet of
      her.

PETRUCHIO.   O monstrous arrogance!
Braved in my own house with a skein of thread!
Away, thou rag, thou quantity, thou remnant
Or I shall so bemete thee with thy yard
As thou shalt think on prating whilst thou liv'st.
I tell thee, I, that thou hast marred her gown.

GRUMIO.   Your worship is deceved. The gown is made
Just as my master had direction.

PETRUCIO.   Go take it hence; be gone and say no more.

(GRUMIO, *as tailor, fearfully snatches gown and
hurriedly exits.*)

PETRUCHIO.   *(Pleasantly)* Come, come, Kate, sit down.

(KATE *does not stir.* PETRUCHIO, *no longer
pleasant, icily repeats.*)

S i t.   d o w n.

(KATE *stands glowering for a moment and then
sits. Immediately* PETRUCHIO *becomes genial
once more.*)

Some food here! Ho! I know you have a stomach.

(HORTENSIO, *wearing mask of servant, enters
with platter, places it on table and steps back.*
KATE, *who is clearly hungry, makes a move
towards the platter.* PETRUCHIO's *hand reaches
it first, preventing* KATE *from removing the lid.*)

Will you give thanks, sweet Kate, or else shall I?

(Proceeds to say grace while KATE *waits. After a
moment he raises the lid of the platter.)*

What's this? Mutton?

HORTENSIO.   Ay.

PETRUCHIO.   'Tis burnt, and so is all the meat.
What dogs are these! Where is the rascal cook?
How durst you, villains, bring it from the dresser,
And serve it thus to me that love it not?
There, take it to you, trenchers, cups, and all.

*(Sweeps the platter off the table and then turns the
table over in one swift, violent movement.*
HORTENSIO *picks up all the pieces and exits
hurriedly.)*

KATE.   I pray you, husband, be not so disquiet,
The meat was well if you were so contented.

PETRUCHIO.   I tell thee, Kate, 'twas burnt and dried
away,

60

And I expressly am forbid to touch it,
For it engenders choler, planteth anger,
And better 'twere that both of us did fast—
Since of ourselves, ourselves are choleric—
Than feed it with such over-roasted flesh.
Be patient. Tomorrow't shall be mended,
And for this night we'll fast for company.
Come, I will show thee to thy bridal chamber.

(PETRUCHIO *claps his hands twice and after a moment,* HORTENSIO *and* GRUMIO, *still disguised as servants, enter and stand waiting by the door.* PETRUCHIO *gestures in the direction of the bridal chamber.* KATE *hesitates for a moment and then, still composed, moves slowly towards the exit. As she nears the servants, she stops and peers into their faces; i.e.* HORTENSIO's *and* GRUMIO's *masks. Then holding her head erect, she continues her progress out. The two servants look up to* PETRUCHIO *and smile slowly.* PETRUCHIO *returns their smile. Slowly, they turn and follow in the direction of* KATE.

PETRUCHIO *then turns to the audience and, revealing for the first time an overt psychopathic manner, begins to speak.)*

PETRUCHIO. Thus have I politicly begun my reign,
And 'tis my hope to end successfully.
My falcon now is sharp and passing empty,
And till she stoop she must not be full gorged,
For then she never looks upon her lure.
Another way I have to man my haggard,
To make her come and know her keeper's call,
That is, to watch her as we watch these kites
That bate and beat and will not be obedient.
She eat no meat today, nor none shall eat.
Last night she slept not, nor tonight she shall not.
As with the meat, some undeserved fault
I'll find about the making of the bed,
And here I'll fling the pillow, there the bolster,
This way the coverlet, another way the sheets.
Ay, and amid this hurly I intend
That all is done in reverent care of her,
And in conclusion she shall watch all night.
And if she chance to nod I'll rail and brawl

And with the clamour keep her still awake.
And thus I'll curb her mad and headstrong humour.
He that knows better how to tame a shrew,
Now let him speak—'tis charity to show.

(Fade out.)

Lights up: BOY *and* GIRL *shouting simultaneously.*

HE. For Christ's sake, will you shut up!

SHE.   Why? Afraid of what the neighbours might say?
Typical working-class angst.

HE. Don't start all that psychoanalytical crap. My id,
my ego, my angst. My ass!

SHE. *(In check)* You wouldn't be you without the
spite and the four letter words.

HE. Cunt!

SHE.   *(Patronizing)* Go on. . .go on.

HE. Shithead! That's eight letters.

SHE. *(Objective)* God, are you pathetic.

HE. And here comes the patronization—right on
schedule. You're so logical, I'm so infantile. . .

SHE.   And obnoxious!⎞
HE. . . . . . obnoxious.⎠

SHE.   and a bore!⎞
HE. . . . . a bore.⎠Why don't you put it on tape. All
you'd have to do is flip a switch.

(Pause. SHE withdraws.)

SHE.   You really enjoy these sessions, don't you? Your
perversity feeds on them.

HE. *(On the true subject)* Get the fucking halter off my
neck. If I want serfdom, I'll go to Siberia. I'll put
my head on the block. I can see anyone I like!

SHE.   And sleep with anyone you like!?

HE. Look baby, if you walked into a room and saw me
holding hands with a nun, you'd assume I just
polished her off on the font.

SHE. *(Cold)* How odious can you get?

HE. I don't know. Depends how long I live.

SHE.   You can soil yourself as much as you like—with
whomever you like—all I ask is that you don't lie
and play the innocent.

63

HE.   No, but you can screw around as much as you like.

SHE.   I may see men; I may even get to like them, but I don't, in your elegant phrase, 'screw around'. I'm not that ravenous—nor that indiscriminate.

HE.   No, you just have mind-fucks.

SHE.   *(Close to tears)* I don't betray you with every pimply youth that whistles at me in the street.

HE.   *(Defending himself)* I tell you that kid is . . . just a kid. She's just cokes, joke-books and bad rock music.

SHE.   Then why let her do this to us?

HE.   Do what, for Christ's sake? You're the only one that's doing anything, and you've been doing it for months. *(A beat. Self-recognition.)* Do you have any idea how ridiculous you make me feel? Forcing me to adopt attitudes that are just. . . assinine!

SHE.   Do you think I enjoy this? Do you think I want my eyes to look like plum-puddings every morning?

HE.   *(Takes her round)* Oh for God's sake, baby.

SHE.   *(Yielding)* Why do you do it, why?

HE.   *(Trying to cool it)* Look, we can't live in each other's pockets. You don't want the kind of love where people melt into each other like grilled cheese. There's you and there's me. That's one and one.

SHE.   But that makes two, doesn't it?

HE.   Look baby, you know what I feel about you.

SHE.   *(Coldly, breaking away)* Let's not recite the catechisms, shall we? I know what *you* feel and you know what *I* feel—so where does that leave us? I want something I can hold on to. Something I can be sure of. Something I can put in the bank.

HE.   *(Not wanting to start again)* Banks fail.

SHE.   And us? Have we failed to?

HE.   *(After a tell-tale moment, hugs her close)* No, for

Christ's sake, we'll go on forever—like The Merry Widow.

(Physical contact gradually relaxes both of them.)

SHE. *(In the embrace)* Promise me you won't see her again.

(HE *tightens the embrace desperately to avoid the issue.)*

SHE.   Please. Promise.

HE. *(Bursting away)* Can't you see what you're doing?

SHE.   *(Hurt by the suddenness of the rupture)* What am I doing that's so horrible? Asking for a show of loyalty while you insist everything be taken on trust!?

HE   Why the hell can't you take it on trust?

SHE.   Why should I? If you mean what you say, why should I?

HE.   There's that sound again. That bloody rack winching away!

SHE.   If you had any real decency in you. . . .

HE. *(Roused)* You mean 'breeding', don't you? I know all your bloody euphemisms by heart.

SHE.   All right, breeding. Is that such a liability in a person? A little breeding; a little sense of honour; a little sense of, yes laugh your head off, chivalry. Respect for things, for people, for vows. Is it so outrageous to want a life with a little dignity attached?

HE. *(Calm)* I can just see your father singing 'God Save the Queen' with that constipated look of patriotism twisting all the muscles in his stupid face.

SHE. *(Objective)* You are such filth.

HE.   Shit, baby, not filth! You can wash filth, but shit stains and smells and corrodes, and that's what you mean isn't it. I'm the Old Shit-Shoveller From The Smelly Suburbs and you're The Fine Lady that's getting her skirts all messed up.

SHE. *(Studying him)* You do this deliberately. You come close just so you can take aim. Just so you can kick me in the teeth.

HE. *(Repentant)* No. . .no. . .no. . .

SHE. That's your pleasure. That's your high. *(Cries.)*

HE. *(Comforting)* Please, please—don't turn me into that ogre you have in your head. It's not me. It's not. I'm trying to love you. I am.

SHE. *(Through tears)* You're not. You're sick of it. You want it dead. You want me dead.

HE. *(In her arms)* No, no baby. I love you; I love you.

SHE. *(Through tears)* No respect.

HE. *(Trying to jolly her out of it)* Come on; come on. Baby, baby.

(HE *kisses her—forcing her to return. The embrace becomes hot, frantic. They move to the floor. Then in a respite. . .)*

SHE. Will you promise? Will you?

(To obliterate his reaction, HE *pushes further into the kiss; into the physical reality of The Girl.* SHE *stiffens; fights him off. They struggle between passion and contempt. She pulls more forcibly out of the embrace. Instinctively, he slaps her hard. There is a moment of nothing.* SHE *on the floor, looking into his eyes. He tries to make it up with more physical contact. She is an iceberg. Eventually, he releases himself from her. She gathers herself together, moves away from him and lights a cigarette.)*

SHE. *(Incongruously sensible)* Look, this is silly. I mean apart from being hurtful and miserable, it's also silly. What's the point? The biggest waste in the world is trying to change people. You don't want it. I don't want it. Why go on?

HE. *(Clocking the inference)* Sometimes you talk as if we met ten minutes ago—the result of some hideous computer-dating system—and all we have to do is shake hands and say goodnight, and that's it. I know

we don't go back to the Flood, but we do have a
kind of history. Things have happened between
us. We're not strangers.

SHE.   *(After a puff)* Aren't we?

HE.   *(Hot)* No, we're not! I know you inside out.

SHE.   *(Refusing to fall into the pattern)* I think we
should give it a rest.

HE.   Stop talking as if we were a bloody dance-act.

SHE.   We just confuse each other. *You* don't understand;
I don't understand. It's just one big bloody
misunderstanding. Let's take some time out.
Maybe it will clear itself up.

HE.   *(Pause)* Is that your gracious way of saying bugger
off.

SHE.   No. It's trying to deal sensibly with a situation
that's becoming nonsensical. You have to admit it
is.

HE.   I don't have to admit anything, and don't hose me
down with all that 'sweet reason' like I was some
kind of head-case.

SHE.   You see what I mean. You *think* that but I don't
mean that.

HE.   Look. . . .

SHE.   One of us has to be sensible.

HE.   And sure enough, it'll be you. Your reliable old
level-headedness will come galloping to the rescue.

SHE.   *(Non-combative)* I'm not going to fight with you.

HE.   *(Getting close)* Look, I'm sorry about that.
(Referring to the slap.) And as for the other thing,
it's not what you think at all. Not at all.

SHE.   *(Pacific)* It doesn't matter. Really.

HE.   *(Despising her cool)* It mattered a helluva lot five
minutes ago.

SHE.   *(Unemotional)* I'm sorry. I was a little hysterical.

HE.   Let's not play The Sorry Game because you know

I always wind up sorrier than you.

SHE.   *(Utterly reasonable)* I don't want to play any
game. *(Checks watch.)* I have to make an early
start tomorrow.

(HE *scoffs to himself, remembering when he heard
that line before.)*

HE.   *(Hungry)* Stay tonight.

SHE.   *(Not wanting to be cruel)* No, not tonight.

HE.   *(Sorry* HE *weakened)* I'm not going to beg,
dammit.

SHE.   I don't expect you to. *(Pause. Cigarette out.)* I
better go.

HE.   *(Tries to stop her with a move)* Look. . .

(SHE *stops, fully composed, looks.)*

HE.   *(After a pause; no more moves to play)* You better
go.

(SHE *kisses him lightly, meaninglessly on the
cheek, and moves off.)*

HE.   *(When she's gone)* I'll call you.

(Fade out.)

Lights up. KATE, *her head on her arm, slumped over table.* GRUMIO *sits whittling across from her. After a moment,* KATE *awakens, looks around, remembers where she is. Her face is white with hunger. Her wedding-dress, in tatters.*

KATE.   What, did he marry me to famish me?
        Beggars that come unto my father's door,
        Upon entreaty have a present alms;
        If not, elsewhere they meet with charity.
        But I, who never knew how to entreat
        Nor never needed that I should entreat,
        Am starved for meat, giddy for lack of sleep,
        With oaths kept waking and with brawling fed.

(Suddenly sees GRUMIO *sitting opposite.)*

        I prithee go and get me some repast,
        I care not what, so it be wholesome food.

GRUMIO.   *(Facing away from her)*
        What say you to a neat's foot?

KATE.   I prithee let me have it.

GRUMIO.   I fear it is too choleric a meat.
        How say you to a fat tripe finely broiled?

KATE.   I like it well. Good Grumio, fetch it me.

GRUMIO.   I cannot tell, I fear 'tis choleric.
        What say you to a piece of beef and mustard?

KATE.   A dish that I do love to feed upon.

GRUMIO.   Ay, but the mustard is too hot a little.

KATE.   Why then, the beef, and let the mustard rest.

GRUMIO.   Nay then, I will not. You shall have the
        mustard
        Or else you get no beef of Grumio.

KATE.   Then both or one, or anything thou wilt.

GRUMIO.   *(Turns full to* KATE)
        Why then, the mustard without the beef.

KATE.   *(Realizing she has been cruelly toyed with)*
        Go, get thee gone, thou false deluding slave,

That feed'st me with the very name of meat.
Sorrow on thee and all the pack of you
That triumph thus upon my misery.
Go, get thee gone, I say.

(Enter PETRUCHIO *and* HORTENSIO *with meat.)*

PETRUCHIO.   How fares my Kate? What, sweeting, all
        amort?

(PETRUCHIO *gives* GRUMIO *his next disguise; a
wig and stick.* GRUMIO *nods and quietly slips
out.)*

HORTENSIO.   Mistress, what cheer?

KATE.   Faith, as cold as can be.

PETRUCHIO.   Pluck up thy spirits; look cheerfully upon
        me.
Here, love, thou seest how diligent I am
To dress thy meat myself and bring it thee.
I am sure, sweet Kate, this kindness merits thanks.
What, not a word? Nay then, thou lov'st it not,
And all my pains is sorted to no proof.
Here, take away this dish.

(HORTENSIO *begins to remove dish;* KATE
desperately lurches towards it.)

KATE.   I pray you, let it stand.

PETRUCHIO.   The poorest service is repaid with thanks,
And so shall mine before you touch the meat.

KATE.   *(Glowering, consumed with hatred, forcing
herself to mouth the words)*
I thank you, sir.

HORTENSIO.   Signior Petruchio, fie, you are to blame.
Come, Mistress Kate, I'll bear you company.

(Sits and begins eating. KATE *suddenly pulled up
and away from table by* PETRUCHIO.)

PETRUCHIO.   And now, my honey love,
Will we return unto thy father's house
And revel it as bravely as the best,
With silken coats and caps and golden rings,
With ruffs and cuffs and fardingales and things,

With scarves and fans and double change of
  brav'ry,
With amber bracelets, beads, and all this knav'ry.

(HORTENSIO *having consumed chicken leg tosses
it to floor. It lands at* PETRUCHIO's *feet.*)

PETRUCHIO.   What, hast thou dined?

(PETRUCHIO *kicks the bone off just as a
desperate* KATE *makes a lurch to pick it up.*)

PETRUCHIO.   Well, come, my Kate, we will unto your
  father's,
Even in these honest mean habiliments.
Our purses shall be proud, our garments poor,
For 'tis the mind that makes the body rich,
And as the sun breaks through the darkest clouds
So honour peereth in the meanest habit.
(To HORTENSIO) Go call my men, and let us
  straight to him;
And bring our horses unto Long-lane end.
There will we mount, and thither walk on foot.
Let's see, I think 'tis now some seven o'clock,
And well we may come there by dinnertime.

KATE.   I do assure you, sir, 'tis almost two,
And 'twill be suppertime ere you come there.

PETRUCHIO.   It shall be seven ere I go to horse.
Look what I speak or do or think to do,
You are still crossing it. Sirs, let't alone:
I will not go today, and ere I do,
It shall be what o'clock I say it is.

(PETRUCHIO *deliberately sits himself down and
stubbornly stares straight ahead.* HORTENSIO,
*realizing his master must be humoured, does like-
wise.* KATE *regards the two immobile men sitting
stock still and facing outward. It all becomes too
much for her. She slumps onto her stool, her head
falling onto her arm on the table.* PETRUCHIO,
*retaining his posture, darts a look at her from the
corner of his eye, then returns to his obdurate
pose. Then, without warning, jumps up gaily and
begins trotting as if he were on horseback.*)

PETRUCHIO.   Come on, in God's name, once more to
  our father's.

(HORTENSIO rises, pulls KATE up from her stool, and places her between PETRUCHIO and himself. Then HORTENSIO also begins to trot in place as if on horseback. KATE, bewildered, regards both men. HORTENSIO makes a sign to her that she should humour PETRUCHIO by trotting as well. After a moment, KATE, who is confused and exhausted, makes a feeble effort to trot along with the two men.)

PETRUCHIO.   Good Lord, how bright and goodly shines
      the moon.

KATE.   The moon? The sun. It is not moonlight now.

PETRUCHIO.   I say it is the moon that shines so bright.

KATE.   I know it is the sun that shines so bright.

PETRUCHIO.   *(Frantic outburst)*
      Now, by my mother's son, and that's myself,
      It shall be moon or star or what I list,
      Or ere I journey to your father's house.
      (To HORTENSIO*)*
      Go on and fetch our horses back again.

(Stops trotting and angrily walks off brooding and smouldering.)

Evermore crossed and crossed, nothing but crossed!

HORTENSIO.   *(To* KATE*)* Say as he says or we shall
      never go.

KATE.   *(Confused)*
      Forward, I pray, since we have come so far,
      And be it moon or sun or what you please.

(PETRUCHIO debates silently for a moment, then trots back to his position and continues to trot in place. HORTENSIO and KATE restored to their imaginary horses beside him.)

PETRUCHIO.   I say it is the moon.

KATE.   I know it is the moon.

PETRUCHIO.   Nay, then you lie. It is the blessèd sun.

KATE.   Then God be blessed, it is the blessèd sun.
      But sun it is not when you say it is not,

And the moon changes even as your mind.
What you will have it named, even that it is,
And so it shall be so for Katherine.

PETRUCHIO.   Well, forward, forward! Thus the bowl
      should run
And not unluckily against the bias.

*(The three continue to trot in place; KATE,
painfully, heavily.)*

But soft, company is coming here.

(Enter GRUMIO now disguised as an old man.)

Good morrow, gentle mistress; where away?
Tell me, Sweet Kate, and tell me truly too,
Hast thou beheld a fresher gentlewoman?
Such war of white and red within her cheeks!
What stars do spangle heaven with such beauty
As those two eyes become that heavenly face?
Fair lovely maid, once more good day to thee.
Sweet Kate, embrace her for her beauty's sake.

KATE.   *(To* GRUMIO, *after a helpless look to* HORTENSIO)
Young budding virgin, fair and fresh and sweet,
Whither away, or where is thy abode?
Happy the parents of so fair a child!
Happier the man whom favourable stars
Allots thee for his lovely bedfellow!

PETRUCHIO.   Why, how now, Kate, I hope thou are
      not mad.
This is a man, old, wrinkled, faded, withered,
And not a maiden, as thou sayst he is.

KATE.   Pardon, old father, my mistaking eyes
That have been so bedazzled with the sun
That everything I look on seemeth green.
Now I perceive thou art a reverend father;
Pardon, I pray thee, for my mad mistaking.
(Falls to her knees, weeping)

PETRUCHIO.   Do, good old grandsire, and withal make
      known
Which way thou travelest. If along with us,
We shall be joyful of thy company.

GRUMIO.   Fair sir, and you my merry mistress,

That with your strange encounter much amazed me,
My name is called Antonia, my dwelling, Verona.

(To PETRUCHIO, *while stripping off his wig and beard, unseen by* KATE *who is at his feet.)*

And bound I am to Padua, there to visit
A son of mine which long I have not seen.

PETRUCHIO.   What is his name?

GRUMIO.   Petruchio, gentle sir.

PETRUCHIO.   Happily met. Come ride with us.

(PETRUCHIO, HORTENSIO *and* GRUMIO *proceed to trot in place, facing straight out. Slowly* PETRUCHIO *turns to the trotting* GRUMIO *and smiles at him;* GRUMIO *smiles back.* PETRUCHIO *then turns and smiles to* HORTENSIO, *who also smiles back. The three continue trotting in place and then trot out.* KATE, *on the floor, pathetically paddles her hands on the floor as if accompanying them in their trot.*

Slowly, KATE *draws herself up. A high-pitched crescendo whistle is heard inside her head which the audience also hears. It builds to an impossible pitch and then something snaps. All lights go red.)*

BAPTISTA.   Poor girl, she weeps.

(Takes KATE *round consolingly.)*

Seeing too much sadness hath congealed your
        blood
And melancholy is the nurse of frenzy.
Until the tears that thou hath lately shed.
Like envious flood o'errun thy lovely face,
Thou wast the finest creature in the world.

GRUMIO.   *(Kindly, as servant)*
Will't please you drink a cup of sack?

HORTENSIO.   *(Kindly, as servant)*
Will't please you taste of these conserves?

GRUMIO.   What raiment will my mistress wear today?
(Puts golden raiment around her shoulders)

74

KATE. *(Looking around)*
Or do I dream or have I dreamed till now?

GRUMIO. Will't thou have music. Hark Apollo plays.

(Harp music faintly in the background.)

And twenty caged nightingales do sing.

HORTENSIO. Or will't thou sleep? We'll have thee to a
couch
Softer and sweeter than the lustful bed
On purpose trimmed up for Semiramis.

BAPTISTA. *(Taking her in his arms)*
Call home thy ancient thoughts from banishment
And banish hence these abject lowly dreams.
Look how thy servants do attend on thee,
Each in his office ready at thy beck.

GRUMIO. Say thou wilt walk, we will bestrow the ground.

HORTENSIO. Or wilt thou ride? Thy horses shall be
trapped
Their harness studded with all gold and pearl.

GRUMIO. Dost thou love pictures? We will fetch thee
straight
Adonis painted by a running brook
And Cytherea all in sedges hid,
Which seems to move and wanton with her breath
Even as the waving sedges play with wind.

KATE. I do not sleep. I see, I hear, I speak.
I smell sweet savors and I feel soft things.

BAPTISTA. O how we joy to see your wit restored.
O that once more you knew but what you are.

KATE. *(Tearful in gratitude)*
The Lord be thanked for thy good amends.

(Enter PETRUCHIO)

PETRUCHIO. *(Kindly)* Where is my wife?

KATE. Here, noble lord. What is thy will with her?

PETRUCHIO. *(Kindly)*
Are you my wife and will not call me husband?

My men call me 'lord'; I am your goodman.

KATE.   My husband and my lord, my lord and husband.
I am your wife in all obedience.

PETRUCHIO.   *(Comes forward, takes her in his arms and
kisses her tenderly)*
Madam, undress you and come now to bed.

KATE.   *(Suddenly fearful)*
Let me entreat of you
To pardon me yet for a night or two,
Or, if not so, until the sun be set.
My physicians have expressly charged
In peril to incur a former malady,
That I should yet absent me from your bed.
I hope this reason stands for my excuse.

*(There is a pause as PETRUCHIO's kindliness
slowly evaporates, and everyone else follows suit.
Slowly, KATE turns from one to the other seeing
only grim and cruel faces on all sides.)*

BAPTISTA.   *(Suddenly fierce)* O monstrous arrogance!

*(KATE is backed over to the table and then thrown
down over it. Her servants and BAPTISTA hold her
wrists to keep her secure. PETRUCHIO looms up
behind her and whips up her skirts ready to do
buggery. As he inserts, an ear-piercing, electronic
whistle rises to a crescendo pitch. KATE's mouth
is wild and open, and it appears as if the impossible
sound is issuing from her lungs.*

Black out)

Lights up on a surreal tribunal-setting. PETRUCHIO *sits
behind a high tribunal-desk. He is looking straight ahead.
In the background, there is the unmistakeable murmur of
women's voices; chatting, gossiping, conniving. After a
moment* GRUMIO, *dressed in a black gown like an official
of the Court, bangs his staff three times. The whispering
stops.*

KATE *is ushered in by* BAPTISTA. *She is wearing a
simple, shapeless instutional-like garment. She stares
straight ahead and gives the impression of being mesmerized. Her face is white; her hair drawn back; her eyes
wide and blank.*

KATE. *(Weakly)*
   What is your will, sir, that you send for me?

PETRUCHIO.   Katherine, I charge thee, tell these head-
             strong women
   What duty they owe to their lords and husbands.

(KATE does not reply. After a moment, BAPTISTA,
*who is beside her, touches her shoulder comfortingly.
Eventually,* KATE *begins to mouthe words. Obviously,
she has learned this speech by rote and is delivering
it as if the words were being spoken by another.)*

KATE. *(Beginning mechanically)*
   Fie, fie, unknit that threatening unkind brow
   And dart not scornful glances from those eyes
   To wound thy lord, thy king, thy governor.
   A woman moved is like a fountain troubled,
   Muddy, ill-seeming, thick, bereft of beauty,
   And while it is so, none so dry or thirsty
   Will deign to sip or touch one drop of it.
   Thy husband is thy lord, thy life, thy keeper,
   Thy head, thy sovereign. . .

*(KATE comes to a dead halt. Her head slumped
onto her chest.* BAPTISTA *steps forward and
shakes her back to life. As soon as she has resumed,
he steps back.)*

   . . . one that cares for thee,
   And for thy maintenance commits his body
   To painful labour both by sea and land,
   To watch the night in storms, the day in cold
   Whilst thou li'st warm at home, secure and safe.

Such duty as the subject owes the prince. . .

(KATE cannot complete the phrase; after a moment, PETRUCHIO prompts her.)

PETRUCHIO.   Even such a woman oweth . . .

KATE. *(Forcing herself on)*
Even such a woman oweth to her husband,
And when she is froward, peevish, sullen, sour,
And not obedient to his honest will,
What is she but a foul contending rebel
And graceless traitor to her loving lord?

(A thump on the table from PETRUCHIO brings KATE, who has reached an hysterical point, back to some semblance of calm.)

I am ashamed that women are so simple
To offer war where they should kneel for peace,
Or seek for rule, supremacy and sway,
When they are bound to serve, love and. . .

(Again KATE cannot frame the word.)

PETRUCHIO. *(Quietly)*. . . obey.

KATE. *(Suddenly frantic)*
Come, come you froward and unable worms,
My mind hath been as big as one of yours,
My heart as great, my reason haply more,
To bandy word for word and frown for frown.
But now I see our lances are but straws,
Our strength, as weak, our weakness, past
          compare,
That seeming to be most which we indeed least
          are.

(From the background, the BOY and GIRL, now dressed in formal wedding attire—he in a dress-suit, she in gleaming white—begin to move toward each other, between PETRUCHIO's tribunal-table and KATE's downstage position.)

KATE.   Then vail your stomachs, for it is no boot,
And place your hands below your husband's foot,
In token of which duty, if he please,
My hand is ready, may it do him ease.

(The bride and bridegroom, now beside each other and framed just behind KATE, *incline their heads to one another and smile out to invisible photographers for a wedding picture.*

Black out.)